atiom

ck

ra

sts
api

the ESe

ELEM~~ent~~ anim

THE
UNIVERSE
ROCKS

RAMAN PRINJA

QED Publishing

THE
UNIVERSE
ROCKS

To Kamini, Vikas and Sachin

Editorial and Design: Windmill Books Ltd.
Illustrator (activities): Geraint Ford/The Art Agency

Copyright © QED Publishing 2012

First published in the UK in 2012 by
QED Publishing, a Quarto Group company
230 City Road
London EC1V 2TT

www.qed-publishing.co.uk

A catalogue record for this book is available from the
British Library.

ISBN 978 1 84835 934 5

Printed in China

Picture credits (t=top, b=bottom, l=left, c=centre,
fc=front cover)
Corbis: Mike Agliol 37br; NASA: 36bl, 42bl, 47tr, 22bl,
28-29, Apollo Gallery 11tr, GRIN 52-53, Hubble Site 48-49,
JPL 30-31, 30l, 33t, 35tr, 40-41t, 40bl, 41b, 43tr, 45t, 46-47,
Caltech/T.Pyle 32-33, 49r, 60-61, 64-65, Li Gang/Xinhua
Press 99t; **ESA**: 12-13, Cassini Huygens 90t; **ESO**: Iztok
Boncina 80-81; **MPIfR**: Jodrell Bank Centre for Astrophysics,
University of Manchester 95t, HSF/ISS Imagery: 86-87, 87tr,
99cl, 100-101t, Hubble Site: 79tr, 84-85, JPL 90-91, NIX 84bl,
85tr, 89t, 102-103, Pat Rawlings/Image of the Day Gallery
Exploration Imagery 92-93, Science News 96-97; **NASA**: 6-7,
4bl, 8-9, 9tr, 12bl, GRIN 32-33, Hubble Site 1t, 8l, 9r, 13tr,
14bl, 14-15, 15br, 22-23, 23br, 26bl, JPL 16-17t, NIX 5, 55r,
62-63, 68bl, 75br, 66-67; GSC 72bl, GRIN 68-69, 74-75,
78-79, Apollo Gallery 92bl, GRIN 86b, 98-99, 99br; Hubble
Site 54-55, 59, 62bl, 73br, 75t, 78-79, 106-107, 67tr, 74t;
NOAA: 18tr, 72-73; **Science Photolibrary**: Chris Butler
18-19, Emilio Segre Visual Archives/American Institute
of Physics 22bl, Mark Garlick 28-29, Mehau Kulyk 26-27,
Detlev Van Ravensway 29bl, Detlev Van Ravensway 36-37,
Richard Bizley 57tr, Chris Butler 56-57, John Chumack
74bl, Lynette Cook 61t Eckhard Stawik 54bl, RIA Novosti
98bl, Detlev Van Ravensway 97; **Shutterstock**: 18-19b, 21t,
Viktar Malyshchyts 4-5, Sander Van Sinttruye 10-11, 50bl,
Marcel Clemens 31t, Elenaphotos 21 42-43, RZ Design 39tr,
63tr, 76, 77b, Andrea Danti 66l, Dan Lonut Popescu
77bl, R Valentina 77tc, 77tr, Guido Brola 71, Paulo Afonso
79br, Vinicius Tupinamba 83; **Thinkstock**: istockphoto 25t,
Guan Kehng Toh 50-51, Rick Whitacre 51br; **W.M. Keck
Observatory**/Rick Peerson: 81tr

*We have made every attempt to contact the copyright
holder. If anyone has any information please contact
smortimer@windmillbooks.co.uk*

Website information is correct at time of going to press.
However, the publishers cannot accept liability for
any information or links found on any Internet sites,
including third-party websites.

In preparation of this book, all due care has been
exercised with regard to the activities and advice
depicted. The publishers regret that they can accept no
liability for any loss or injury sustained.

Words in **bold**
are explained in
the glossary on
page 115

What is a light-year?

Distances in space are measured in light-years.
A light-year is the distance that light travels in one year.
• In one second light travels 300,000 kilometres
  – or around Earth seven times.
• In one minute light travels 18 million kilometres
  – or to the Moon and back 50 times.
• In one year light travels 9000 billion kilometres
  – or one light-year.

CONTENTS

WELCOME TO THE MILKY WAY

The Sun and all the stars you see at night belong to our home **galaxy**, which we call the Milky Way. A galaxy is an enormous collection of billions of stars, plus gas and dust held together by **gravity**.

There are **billions** of galaxies in the **Universe**. In this book we will journey to some amazing galaxies, watch enormous crashes in space, and learn about the latest mysteries of the Universe.

Seen from the side, the Milky Way Galaxy is a thin disc with a bulge in the middle.

The Milky Way

Our home

From above, our Milky Way Galaxy would look like a giant pinwheel, with long arms of stars and **dust** clouds. From the side it looks a bit like two fried eggs stuck back to back! The Sun is just one of 200 billion stars in our Galaxy. Astronomers think that an enormous **black hole**, with 3 million times more mass than the Sun, is at the heart of the Milky Way.

Light-years across

The Universe is so vast that the sizes and distances between galaxies are hard to imagine. Instead of using kilometres to measure distance, **astronomers** use a unit called a **light-year**. One light-year is the distance light travels in a **year**. That is about 9000 billion kilometres! The Milky Way Galaxy is so big that light would take 100,000 years to travel from one side to the other. We say that the Milky Way Galaxy is 100,000 light-years across.

> The bright bulge in the middle of the Milky Way is packed with lots of stars.

Scaling it down

We can use scale models to help understand the huge sizes of galaxies. Imagine the Sun is the size of a grain of sand. The Earth would be an even tinier speck about 1 centimetre away from the grain. Even in this tiny model, the Milky Way Galaxy, with its 200 billion stars (or grains of sand), would still be 80,000 kilometres across. That's six times wider than the Earth's diameter!

GALAXY ALL-SORTS

Galaxies don't all have the same size or shape. There are dwarf galaxies made of millions of stars and giant galaxies loaded with trillions of them.

The sizes of galaxies can be between a few thousand light-years across to several hundred thousand light-years. In the 1920s an astronomer called Edwin Hubble studied lots of galaxies and found that they looked different. There are three main types of galaxies, called **spirals**, ellipticals and irregulars.

This spiral galaxy looks like ours. The Sun would be about here.

Spirals

Our Milky Way Galaxy is a spiral galaxy. Most of the stars, gas and dust clouds are gathered in arms that wind out from the centre of a galaxy. The whole galaxy spins like a giant whirlpool. Spiral galaxies have lots of new stars in them. About a fifth of all galaxies in the Universe are spirals.

Ellipticals

Elliptical galaxies are shaped like rugby balls. These galaxies are mostly made up of old stars and have much less dust than spiral galaxies. The largest galaxies in the Universe are ellipticals with **trillions** of stars.

An irregular 'messy' galaxy!

Elliptical galaxy surrounded by many other distant galaxies.

Irregulars

Irregular galaxies don't have any real shape. They look like messy collections of stars, gas and dust. Irregular galaxies are usually the smallest and have lots of bright, newly born stars in them.

Imaginary view of a Quasar.

Powering up

Some of the most energetic galaxies in the Universe are called **quasars**. They are also among the farthest galaxies we can see in the Universe. Quasars are so far away that the light from them can take 10 billion years to reach us!

BUILD YOUR OWN MILKY WAY

The Milky Way is a spiral of stars, gas and dust. In this activity you can make your own model of our Galaxy.

The Milky Way can be seen in the night sky as a misty band of light, full of stars.

TRY DOING THIS...

Find out about the shape of our Galaxy and the place of our Solar System inside it.

You will need:

* 30 cm diameter plate
* Thick black card
* Pencil
* Scissors
* PVA glue
* Cotton wool balls
* Silver and blue glitter
* Red dot stickers
* String

1 Place the 30 centimetre plate on the black card and draw around the plate. You will have a large circle. Ask an adult to use the scissors to cut out the circle.

Ask an adult to help.

30cm

2 Glue some cotton wool balls in the centre of the card. Use enough to cover a space 8 centimetres across. Glue more balls onto the other side of the card. You should have a dome shaped bulge at the centre.

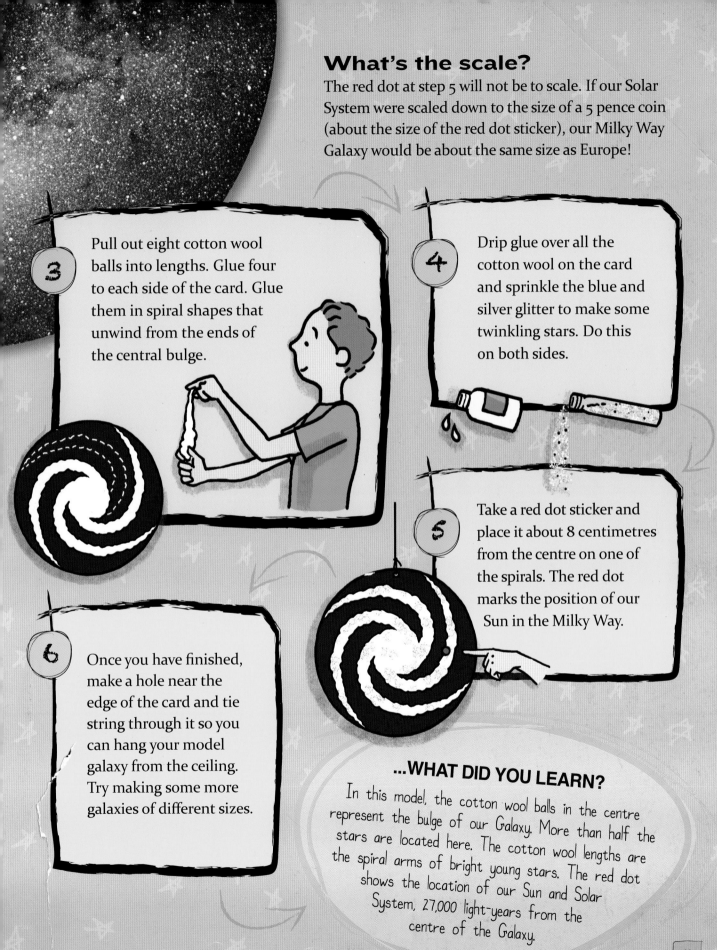

What's the scale?

The red dot at step 5 will not be to scale. If our Solar System were scaled down to the size of a 5 pence coin (about the size of the red dot sticker), our Milky Way Galaxy would be about the same size as Europe!

3 Pull out eight cotton wool balls into lengths. Glue four to each side of the card. Glue them in spiral shapes that unwind from the ends of the central bulge.

4 Drip glue over all the cotton wool on the card and sprinkle the blue and silver glitter to make some twinkling stars. Do this on both sides.

5 Take a red dot sticker and place it about 8 centimetres from the centre on one of the spirals. The red dot marks the position of our Sun in the Milky Way.

6 Once you have finished, make a hole near the edge of the card and tie string through it so you can hang your model galaxy from the ceiling. Try making some more galaxies of different sizes.

...WHAT DID YOU LEARN?

In this model, the cotton wool balls in the centre represent the bulge of our Galaxy. More than half the stars are located here. The cotton wool lengths are the spiral arms of bright young stars. The red dot shows the location of our Sun and Solar System, 27,000 light-years from the centre of the Galaxy.

MAPPING THE UNIVERSE

There may be 200 billion galaxies in the Universe. Scientists are using powerful telescopes to make a map showing how they are all positioned in space.

Galaxies are mostly found in groups, where dozens are held together by gravity. Imagine that you are a **planet**, and your house is a solar system – the other people in your family are other planets. Then you can think of your home city or town as a galaxy of houses. On a map of your country, the cities are different galaxies and the countryside between them is like the empty space between galaxies.

Gravity holds galaxies together, even across thousands of light-years of empty space.

Andromeda

Meet the neighbours

The Milky Way is part of a group of 35 galaxies that includes another magnificent spiral galaxy called Andromeda. This group of galaxies is spaced out over a vast distance of about 5 million light-years. There are many other similar groups of galaxies in space.

Spongy Universe

Galaxies are not evenly spread across the Universe. The galaxies form chains that run between large bubbles of space that are almost empty. The pattern made by galaxies is a bit like the holes in a bath sponge!

Biggest things in the Universe

Astronomers have mapped out where the galaxies are in the Universe and discovered some amazing structures. They have found that some groups of galaxies can be linked to make enormous stretched-out chains across space. Known as **superclusters**, these groups of galaxies can stretch over distances of more than 100 million light-years. Superclusters of galaxies are the largest things in the Universe. They can contain 2,000 large galaxies and 50,000 smaller ones. That all adds up to 200 trillion stars in a supercluster!

COSMIC CRASHES

Sometimes the force of gravity can bring pairs of galaxies so close that they crash together!

Large galaxies gobble up smaller ones and grow even bigger. Galaxy crashes can take hundreds of millions of years to happen, so we can't watch a full collision from start to finish. Instead astronomers use powerful telescopes to take photographs of galaxies in the process of coming together in space.

Galaxy smash

Antennae galaxies

The Hubble Space Telescope has taken fantastic images of two galaxies that started to crash into each other a few hundred million years ago. Called the Antennae galaxies, these spiral galaxies are 75 million light-years away from us. As the galaxies crash in a head-on collision, their clouds of gas and dust get crushed together and many new stars are made.

These colliding galaxies are called the Mice because they both have long tails.

Heading for a crash!

The Milky Way and the Andromeda Galaxy are on a collision course in space. But don't worry – it won't start happening for another 3 billion years! Today the two galaxies are more than 2 million light-years apart. But they are heading towards each other at a speed of 500,000 kilometres per hour.

There is a lot of empty space in galaxies, and the stars are far apart. Scientists think that millions of years after the crash starts, the two galaxies will eventually join into one enormous galaxy.

The bright blue rim around the Cartwheel Galaxy is a ring of new stars.

Fiery cartwheel

Another head-on collision, 500 million light-years away, has made the Cartwheel Galaxy. A smaller galaxy plunged into the middle of a larger one. Just like ripples when a rock is thrown into a pond, the crash made a wave of gas move out from the centre of the larger galaxy. The waves swept up more and more gas and squeezed it to make new stars. Two billion newly born stars are seen in a giant ring, or cartwheel, around the galaxy.

GALAXIES IN A CUP

We have learnt that there are three main types of galaxy called spirals, ellipticals and irregulars. Here we explore spiral galaxies.

TRY DOING THIS...

In this activity explore the shape of spiral galaxies and see how the arms can be made as the galaxy spins.

In a spin

Our entire Galaxy is spinning and it takes the Sun almost 225 million years to complete one trip around our Galaxy. The Sun moves at an incredible 792,000 kilometres every hour!

You will need:

* Plastic cups
* Water
* Blue food colouring
* Plastic teaspoons
* Powdered milk

2 Sprinkle about half a teaspoon of powdered milk into the centre of the cup. Look at the spiral-shaped patterns made by the milk powder as it swirls around.

1 Fill three plastic cups half full of water and add a few drops of blue colouring. Carefully lift and turn one cup in circles to make the water swirl around. Put the cup on a table while the water inside is still moving.

Half full

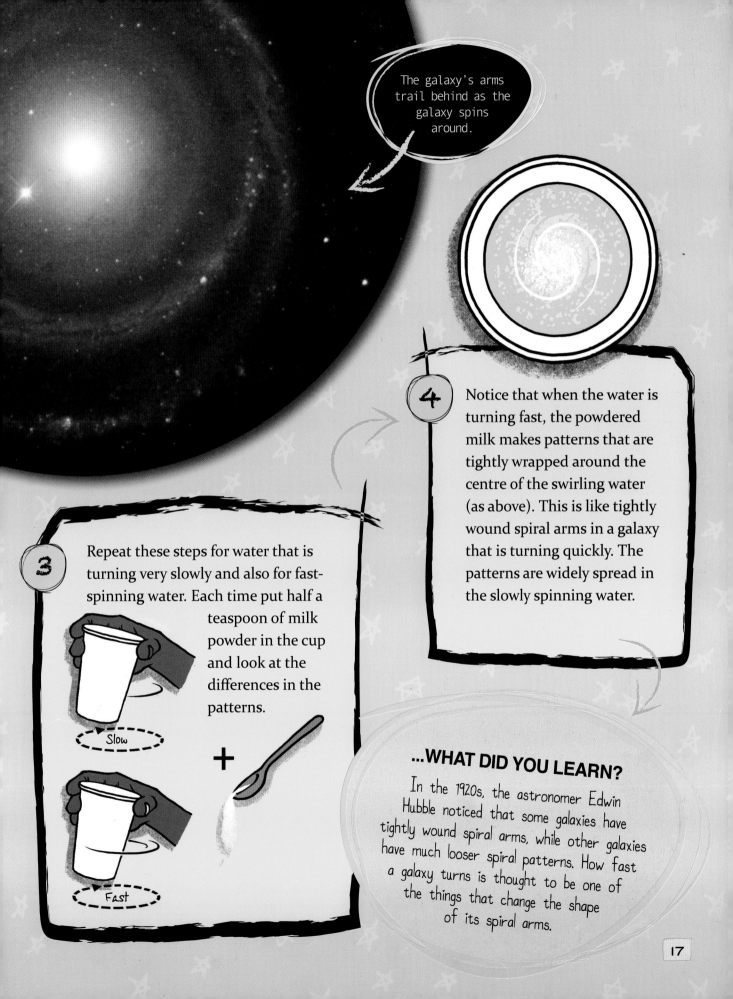

The galaxy's arms trail behind as the galaxy spins around.

4 Notice that when the water is turning fast, the powdered milk makes patterns that are tightly wrapped around the centre of the swirling water (as above). This is like tightly wound spiral arms in a galaxy that is turning quickly. The patterns are widely spread in the slowly spinning water.

3 Repeat these steps for water that is turning very slowly and also for fast-spinning water. Each time put half a teaspoon of milk powder in the cup and look at the differences in the patterns.

Slow

+

Fast

...WHAT DID YOU LEARN?

In the 1920s, the astronomer Edwin Hubble noticed that some galaxies have tightly wound spiral arms, while other galaxies have much looser spiral patterns. How fast a galaxy turns is thought to be one of the things that change the shape of its spiral arms.

It Started With a Big Bang

Astronomers think that the Universe began about 14 billion years ago with a sudden explosion we call the **Big Bang**.

In less than one second the incredibly hot Universe grew from being hundreds of times smaller than a pinhead to bigger than a galaxy. The Universe has kept growing ever since, like a balloon being filled with air. After the Big Bang, as the Universe cooled down, **atoms**, galaxies, stars and planets started to form.

Cosmic year

To understand how the Universe has changed since the Big Bang, let's imagine its 14-billion-year history speeded up so it lasts just one year. Each calendar month equals just over a billion years.

1st January:

The Big Bang

A tiny fraction of a second after the Big Bang, the whole Universe would have fitted inside a grapefruit.

31st March:

The Milky Way Galaxy appears

| January | February | March | April | May | June |

Radio waves

An ancient glow

The Universe cooled down a lot as it grew larger and larger. About 300,000 years after the Big Bang, the Universe was still five times hotter than the Sun. A glow of light was released that is still around today and fills the Universe. This glow is made up of radio waves. The radio waves were detected in the 1950s by two scientists called Arno Penzias and Robert Wilson.

Big Bang

18th December:
Plants start growing on land
24th December:
Dinosaurs start stomping around
29th December: Dinosaurs are extinct
31st December:
All of human history from ancient Egypt to today fits into the last 10 seconds of our **cosmic** year!

31st August:
The Sun and planets form

July	August	September	October	November	December

TIMELINE OF THE UNIVERSE

The Universe has changed over billions of years. Along the way many important events occurred, such as the birth of galaxies, the formation of Earth and the start of life.

TRY DOING THIS...

In this activity you can make a timeline to show how far apart the events in the Universe happened.

You will need:

* 7 index cards (10 x 15 cm)
* Long wall outside (about 35 metres) or a clear floor
* One long roll of paper
* Pack of sticky tack
* Coloured pencils
* Measuring tape

Slow but sure

Changes in space mostly happen very slowly. We have been studying the Universe with powerful telescopes for about a century, but changes in space can take millions or billions of years.

1 On each of the index cards write down one of these seven important events: 'The Big Bang', 'First galaxies', 'Our Sun and the planets', 'Life starting on Earth', 'First dinosaurs', 'First humans', 'History of humans from ancient Egypt to today'. Also make a drawing on each card.

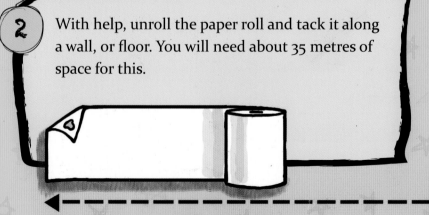

2 With help, unroll the paper roll and tack it along a wall, or floor. You will need about 35 metres of space for this.

35 metres

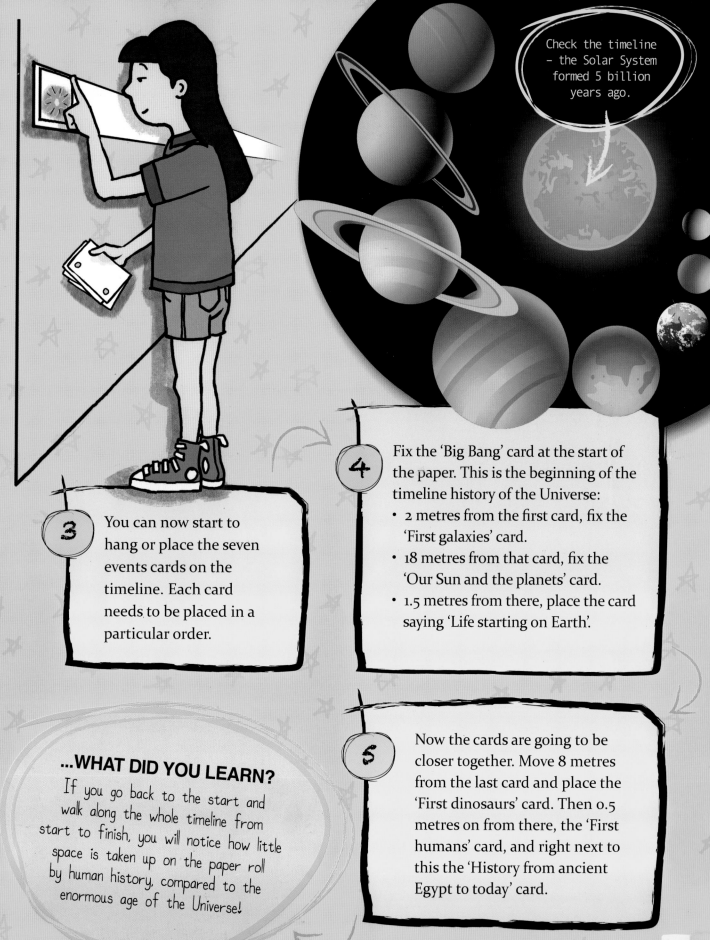

Check the timeline – the Solar System formed 5 billion years ago.

4 Fix the 'Big Bang' card at the start of the paper. This is the beginning of the timeline history of the Universe:
- 2 metres from the first card, fix the 'First galaxies' card.
- 18 metres from that card, fix the 'Our Sun and the planets' card.
- 1.5 metres from there, place the card saying 'Life starting on Earth'.

3 You can now start to hang or place the seven events cards on the timeline. Each card needs to be placed in a particular order.

5 Now the cards are going to be closer together. Move 8 metres from the last card and place the 'First dinosaurs' card. Then 0.5 metres on from there, the 'First humans' card, and right next to this the 'History from ancient Egypt to today' card.

...WHAT DID YOU LEARN?

If you go back to the start and walk along the whole timeline from start to finish, you will notice how little space is taken up on the paper roll by human history, compared to the enormous age of the Universe!

EVERYTHING IS FLYING APART

The Universe has been growing ever since it began. The space we see and explore is billions of times bigger than it was when the Universe was very young.

The further away a galaxy is, the faster it appears to be moving away from us. Imagine the galaxies are raisins in a cake in the oven. As the mixture heats up, it expands and each raisin, or galaxy, moves away from the others.

Edwin Hubble made his discoveries using one of the largest telescopes in the world.

Going for a ride

In the mid-1920s when the astronomer Edwin Hubble looked at the light from galaxies, he noticed something remarkable. Nearly all the galaxies are moving farther away from each other. It's as though the galaxies are going along for a ride as the Universe grows larger. The space between galaxies is getting bigger. Edwin Hubble also discovered that the farthest galaxies are moving away from Earth faster than galaxies that are closer to us.

Age of the Universe

By looking at galaxies flying apart, astronomers know how quickly the Universe is expanding. They can also figure out how long the Universe has been getting bigger. Like playing a film backwards, we can then work out when everything was much closer together, and even when the Universe was born. Scientists think the Universe is about 14 billion years old.

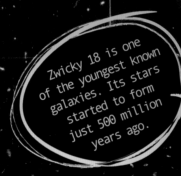

Zwicky 18 is one of the youngest known galaxies. Its stars started to form just 500 million years ago.

The colour of a galaxy tells astronomers about the kinds of stars present, and their ages.

Runaway Universe

As the Universe cooled, tiny atoms formed. Gravity pulled the atoms together to make huge clouds of gas. The gas clumped together to make stars, which gathered into galaxies. Scientists expected that the gravity of all the galaxies would pull on the Universe and make it grow more slowly. But in fact the Universe is getting bigger faster and faster. No one is sure why the Universe is growing so quickly.

BALLOON UNIVERSE

We have seen that ever since the Big Bang about 14 billion years ago, the Universe has continued to swell and expand in all directions.

You will need:

✳ A large balloon

✳ A permanent felt-tip marker pen

TRY DOING THIS...

Make a simple model to understand how the Universe expands and why galaxies move away from each other.

1 10cm — Blow up the balloon just a little until it is about 10 centimetres across. Twist the end so that the air does not come out, but don't tie the end.

Changing views

In ancient times people had very different ideas about the Universe. Almost 2000 years ago the ancient Greeks thought the Earth was at the centre, with all the stars and planets moving around it.

2 Using the felt-tip pen, mark 10 dots on the balloon in different places. The dots represent galaxies and the balloon is the Universe. Mark one of the dots 'MW', for our Milky Way Galaxy.

3 Take note of the distance between the dots on the balloon. You can think of the small balloon being the Universe when it was very young.

Astronomers believe the Universe and everything in it started with a Big Bang.

20cm

MW

4 Blow up the balloon a lot more to make it about 20 centimetres across. Look again at the spacing between the dots. You can think of the larger balloon as the Universe today.

...WHAT DID YOU LEARN?

The dots on the balloon are the galaxies going for a ride with the expanding Universe. Notice how all the dots move away from each other as the balloon gets larger and larger. This is just the way galaxies are moving further and further apart from each other. The bigger the Universe (balloon) grows, the more widely spaced are the galaxies (dots).

MW

5 Now blow up the balloon and make it bigger. You are expanding your model Universe! Twist the end of the balloon again and look at what has happened to the spaces between the dots – or galaxies.

THE DARK SIDE OF THE UNIVERSE

Scientists have found that most of the Universe is so dark and mysterious that we cannot see it even when using powerful telescopes!

More than 90 percent of the Universe is invisible. The vast numbers of galaxies are just a tiny part of it.

In this picture of a cluster of galaxies, suspected dark matter is shown in blue and the galaxies are red.

Dead stars

Almost a quarter of the **matter** in the Universe is hidden from our view **because** it is too small or too cold to shine. Astronomers call this dark matter because we can't see light from it. Dark matter can be stars that have burnt out and died, so they don't shine any more. There may also be lots of cold clouds of gas and dust in space that we just can't see.

Brown dwarf

Really strange energy!

Almost three-quarters of the Universe is in the form of a very strange and mysterious energy called dark energy. No one is sure what this energy is or how it works. Dark energy is one of the amazing new discoveries of space. Astronomers think that dark energy is making the Universe grow faster and faster. We hope one day to understand what dark energy is and how it is pushing the Universe apart.

Strange particles

Scientists think that the Universe is flooded with lots of strange particles that are much smaller even than an atom. Each of these particles has just a tiny mass – almost nothing – but there are so many of them that they could add up to make a large amount of dark matter.

FATE OF THE UNIVERSE

Ever since scientists worked out that the Universe started with a Big Bang, they have wondered how the Universe would end.

If the Universe has lots more matter than we know about, then it might stop growing in the future. The Universe could then start shrinking. Instead of expanding, the Universe could get smaller and smaller. It may close in on itself in a **Big Crunch**. Perhaps a new Big Bang would then start up a new Universe!

Galaxies

Other universes may be bubbles with no way to move between them.

Other universes?

An amazing possibility is that ours is not the only universe. There could be many other universes, each with billions of galaxies and trillions of stars. But we don't know anything about the other universes because we can't look into them.

Big Freeze or Big Rip?

Instead of closing in a crunch, the Universe may instead continue to grow and stretch forever. The farthest galaxies will move even farther away from us. The Universe would get colder as it grew larger and end up in a **Big Freeze** with no heat left at all! Some scientists think that if the Universe is stretched too much by dark energy, even galaxies could start to break apart. Finally planets and even atoms would not be able to stand the stretch of space. This is called the **Big Rip**. But don't worry. If the Big Rip happens it won't start for another 20 billion years from now!

This artist's impression of the Big Crunch shows the Universe shrinking and destroying all stars and galaxies in existence.

TOUR OF THE SOLAR SYSTEM

Our Solar System is made up of a star we call the Sun, eight planets, many dwarf planets, over a hundred moons, millions of rocky **asteroids** and billions of icy **comets**.

Now we will go on a fantastic tour of the Solar System. Our travels will take us from bubbling hot gas on the Sun to **volcanoes** erupting ice and steam on the moons of the outer planets. We will explore the magnificent rings of Saturn and hunt for water beyond Earth.

The Sun

Venus

Mars

Mercury

Earth

Jupiter

Eight worlds

Our Solar System is home to eight planets, the largest objects that **orbit** the Sun. In order of distance from the Sun they are Mercury, Venus, Earth, Mars, Jupiter, Saturn, Uranus and Neptune.

MERCURY Super-hot during the but freezing at night.

VENUS At 450 degrees Celsius th the hottest planet of them all.

EARTH Our home is the only kno where life exists. Oceans of liqu exist on the surface.

Comet

Besides planets there are also smaller objects in the Solar System. There are asteroids made of rock and iron, mostly found between Mars and Jupiter. There are also billions of comets made of rock and ice. As a comet gets close to the Sun, the frozen gases heat up and make huge tails that flow behind the comet.

Saturn

Uranus

Neptune

MARS The red planet has huge mountains and deep canyons. The red colour comes from dust that covers the surface. Mars once had rivers and streams like Earth.

SATURN All the giant gas planets have rings around them, but none are as beautiful and grand as Saturn's rings.

JUPITER This is a giant gas planet – the largest of all – but it has no solid surface to stand on. More than 40 moons circle around Jupiter; some of them are bigger than Mercury.

URANUS Cold methane gas gives Uranus a lovely blue-green colour.

NEPTUNE The farthest planet from the Sun, this gas planet gets very cold.

How the planets were made

The planets, moons, asteroids and comets were made from gas and dust that was left over after the Sun had formed.

The Sun was made about 5 billion years ago out of a giant cloud of gas and dust. Gravity slowly crushed the gas into a large ball that became fiercely hot. The material that was not used formed a disc around the newly born star. Over millions of years specks of dust joined into clumps, which then stuck together to form rocks. The rocks crashed together, very slowly growing into the planets.

Spinning disc of dust

The Sun

Small rocks grew from billions of specks of dust that bashed into each other and stuck together. These are called A asteroids.

Round the Sun
The Sun spins because the cloud it formed from was also spinning. The planets move in the same direction as the star, circling it in paths called orbits. Mercury takes just 88 **days** to complete one lap around the Sun. The Earth takes 365 days and we call this a year. Distant Neptune takes 60,100 days (165 Earth years).

Mercury Venus Earth Mars Jupiter Saturn Uranus Neptune

Spinning tops

The planets also turn like spinning tops. The Earth spins around once in 24 hours and we call this a day. Venus spins more slowly – and in the other direction – taking 243 Earth days to turn once. But a day on Jupiter is very short. The giant planet spins around in just 10 hours!

Outer planets are mainly gas, although some have cores made of ice and rock.

Rocks inside and gas outside

Close to the Sun where the **temperature** is higher, only small rocky planets formed – Mercury, Venus, Earth and Mars. Farther away from the Sun in the outer Solar System, it was much colder and icy material gathered there. The giant planets Jupiter, Saturn, Uranus and Neptune form the outer Solar System. They were big enough to trap lots of gas and make huge, thick **atmospheres**.

TOILET-PAPER SOLAR SYSTEM

The planets in our Solar System are separated by enormous distances.

You will need:

✳ A regular roll of toilet paper (usually more than 200 sheets)
✳ A large room (or outside space)
✳ A felt-tipped pen

TRY DOING THIS...

Here is a simple activity to help you understand just how huge the Solar System is.

What's going on?

Earth is nearly 150 million kilometres away from the Sun, and Jupiter is more than 600 million kilometres from the Earth. The farthest planet, Neptune, is about 5 billion kilometres from the Sun. These huge distances are hard for us to imagine. In this activity you can understand the spacing between planets using a scale made from toilet paper.

1 Mark a dot in the middle of the first sheet of the roll. Label this dot the Sun.

2 You can now start to roll out the sheets slowly, taking care not to rip the paper.

Unroll until you have 90 sheets

SUN

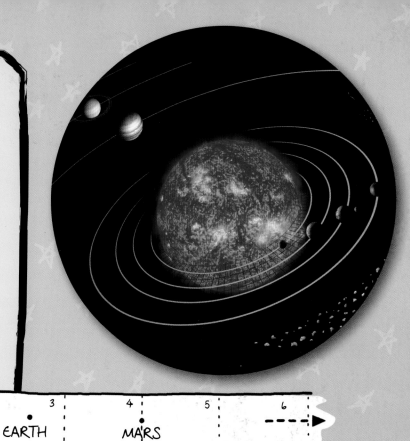

3 Mark the positions and names of the rest of the planets along the unwinding roll, using the numbers in this table:

Planets	Sheets (after first sheet)
Mercury	1
Venus	2
Earth	3
Mars	4.5
Jupiter	15.5
Saturn	29
Uranus	57
Neptune	90

SUN | MERCURY | VENUS | EARTH | MARS

1 2 3 4 5 6

4 Now walk along the toilet roll Solar System. Notice how the first four rocky planets are much closer to the Sun than the giant gas planets. In this scale model you would have to roll out 2 million sheets to mark on the next nearest star!

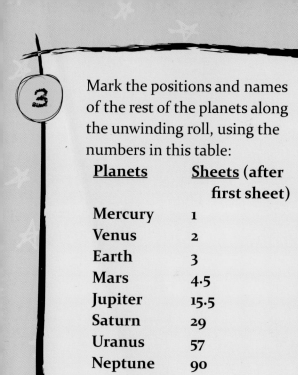

SUN MERCURY VENUS EARTH MARS

In our scale model the length of one sheet of square toilet paper is equal to 50 million kilometres.

...WHAT DID YOU LEARN?

In this activity we have learnt about the different spacing of the paths or orbits of the planets as they go around the Sun. You can try other scale models to explore the different sizes of the planets themselves. For example, imagine the giant planet Jupiter was the size of a basketball. On this very reduced scale, Earth would be the size of a small marble!

FOLLOW THE WATER

Water is very important to us because it makes life on Earth possible.

Living things need water to survive and almost three-quarters of our planet is covered in liquid water as oceans, rivers and lakes. Scientists exploring the Solar System have found water on distant moons and planets. These discoveries are even making people wonder whether simple life-forms, such as **bacteria**, may also be present somewhere else in the Solar System.

Europa is covered in cracks, where the ice is being broken by the movement of water beneath the surface.

Europa

Beneath icy moons

A **spacecraft** called Galileo took close-up pictures of Europa, one of Jupiter's moons. The pictures showed that Europa had water below its frozen surface. Scientists think there could be an ocean 100 kilometres deep hidden beneath the surface. No one knows if life-forms such as bacteria exist in this dark ocean.

In deep craters

Spacecraft sent to orbit Earth's Moon have discovered water ice in the Moon's deep craters. The craters were formed a long time ago when comets and asteroids crashed into the Moon. Parts of some craters always remain in shadow, and are very cold at the bottom. The water in the craters does not form pools or lakes. It is small icy lumps that are mixed with the dust. Water ice has even been found in cold craters on Mercury!

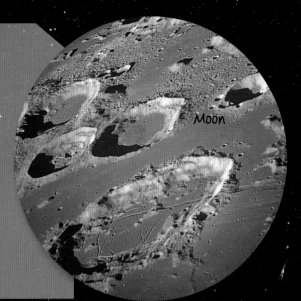

Moon

Comets crash with a big explosion but some of the water they carry freezes back into ice.

Delivered by comets

Comets are the water bearers of the Solar System. A lot of water was carried by comets, which are made from 'dirty snow'. Billions of years ago the comets crashed into the planets and moons, making craters and dropping icy material.

ERUPTING VOLCANO

The surfaces of Earth, Mars and some moons are shaped by volcanoes that spread lots of liquid rock called lava.

TRY DOING THIS...

In this activity, make a mini volcano that has lava made from bubbles instead of red-hot liquid rock.

It's gonna blow!

The Earth still has many active volcanoes on it today, including some fiery ones on the islands of Hawaii in the Pacific Ocean. Mars has not had any active volcanoes for millions of years, but it does have the largest volcanic mountain in the Solar System. Known as Olympus Mons, this mountain on Mars is three times taller than Mount Everest on Earth.

You will need:

* An empty 500 millilitre plastic water bottle
* Large baking tray
* Heap of soil
* A few drops of red food colouring
* 225 millilitres of vinegar in a jug
* 15 millilitres of bicarbonate of soda
* A tablespoon

1 Place the empty water bottle in the middle of the baking tray. Remove the cap from the bottle.

2 Place soil firmly around the bottle to make a mountain shape. Make sure you don't cover the top of the bottle.

3 Add a few drops of red colouring to the vinegar. This will make your version of fiery lava.

Lava cools down once it comes to the surface, forming a new layer of rock.

4 Pour the bicarbonate of soda into the bottle using the spoon.

...WHAT DID YOU LEARN?

When you mixed the vinegar and baking soda in the bottle, they reacted together to make a gas called carbon dioxide. The gas builds up inside the bottle until it forces its way out through the top. Beneath the Earth's crust, magma, a mixture of rock and gases, sometimes does the same thing. It rises up through cracks in rocks and bursts out as lava.

5 Now pour the red-coloured vinegar into the bottle and watch what happens! Red foam will rise up out of the bottle and run down the sides of the soil mountain. You've made an erupting volcano!

ICY VOLCANOES

There are some fantastic wonders in the Solar System and one of the best is volcanoes that blast out ice!

On Earth we see fire and lava pouring from active volcanoes such as Mount Etna in Sicily or on the islands of Hawaii. In the distant Solar System the moons of the giant planets are also covered in volcanoes. But these strange mountains spray out icy rock rather than hot melted rock.

Triton is a dwarf planet that was pulled into Neptune's orbit when the Solar System was young.

Triton

Frozen Triton

One of the coldest places in the Solar System is a moon of Neptune called Triton. The temperature on its surface is -235 degrees Celsius. There are high ridges and deep valleys all over it. A spacecraft called *Voyager 2* flew past Triton and took pictures of active volcanoes. Frozen material was seen rising eight kilometres above Triton's surface. The sprays of fresh ice keep Triton looking white.

The *Cassini* spacecraft flew past Enceladus in 2009. Plumes of ice were seen coming from volcanoes on this ice moon of Saturn.

Welcome to Enceladus

Enceladus is one of Saturn's 53 known moons. It is only 520 kilometres across and is the eighth furthest moon from the giant planet. The *Cassini* spacecraft has taken a close look at Enceladus. The moon has a bright surface covered by fresh, clean ice. Fountains of water ice blast above the surface. The icy eruptions rise up thousands of kilometres.

Titan's mountains

Titan is the largest moon of Saturn. The *Cassini* spacecraft made maps of its surface. The maps show an ice volcano 1500 metres high. The water and **ammonia** ice thrown up by this volcano may have helped Titan build up a thick atmosphere around it.

A 3D computer image of an ice volcano called Sotra Facula on the surface of Titan. The iced-over areas are shown in blue.

SATURN IN THE SPOTLIGHT

Saturn is one of the most beautiful planets in the Solar System, with its magnificent rings and weird moons.

Saturn is the second largest planet in the Solar System. You could fit nearly 750 Earths inside Saturn! But although Saturn is large, it is mostly made of **hydrogen** and **helium** gases. If you could put Saturn in a big enough tank of water, it would float at the top!

Astronomers think Saturn's rings may have been made from a shattered icy moon.

Titan's lakes

Saturn's largest moon, Titan, is the only moon in the Solar System to have a thick atmosphere. Titan is a weird place that has lakes and rivers of oil. The atmosphere is made mainly of nitrogen gas. Scientists are studying Titan because they think it can teach us a lot about how life started on our planet Earth.

Imaginary view of Titan

Saturn

Storms brewing

There are many raging storms and fierce winds blowing on Saturn. **Hurricanes** at its north pole can be 14,000 kilometres long. There are also lightning storms that last up to six months. They fire bolts of energy that are 10,000 times more powerful than those found on Earth. Near Saturn's **equator**, the speeds of the winds can reach 1,800 kilometres per hour, while the strongest hurricanes on Earth blow at 400 kilometres per hour.

Lord of the Rings

All four giant gas planets – Jupiter, Saturn, Uranus and Neptune – have rings around them. But none are as large, bright and beautiful as those of Saturn. The *Cassini* spacecraft beamed back fantastic pictures of Saturn's rings to Earth. The rings are made up of billions of pieces of ice. The frozen bands include tiny ice grains as well as lumps the size of mountains. End-to-end, Saturn's rings stretch 280,000 kilometres. That is three-quarters of the distance from the Earth to the Moon.

CD SATURN

Among the most majestic sights in space are the amazing rings of the gas planet Saturn.

You will need:

* An unwanted CD
* Gold and silver glitter
* Small polystyrene ball (about 5 centimetres across)
* Brush-on glue
* Wooden toothpicks
* Scissors
* Paper clip

Distinctive shape

No other planet looks like Saturn. Even early astronomers who looked at it with simple telescopes could see the rings, which stretch out either side. In this activity you can make your own version of the ringed planet.

1 The CD will be used as the rings of Saturn. On one side of the CD use the brush to carefully spread some glue. Avoid the centre part of the CD.

3 Ask an adult to cut the polystyrene ball in half. A sharp knife may be needed for this.

Ask an adult to help.

2 Sprinkle the silver and gold glitter on the wet glue and let it dry fully.

4 Stick one toothpick into the flat side of each half of the ball.

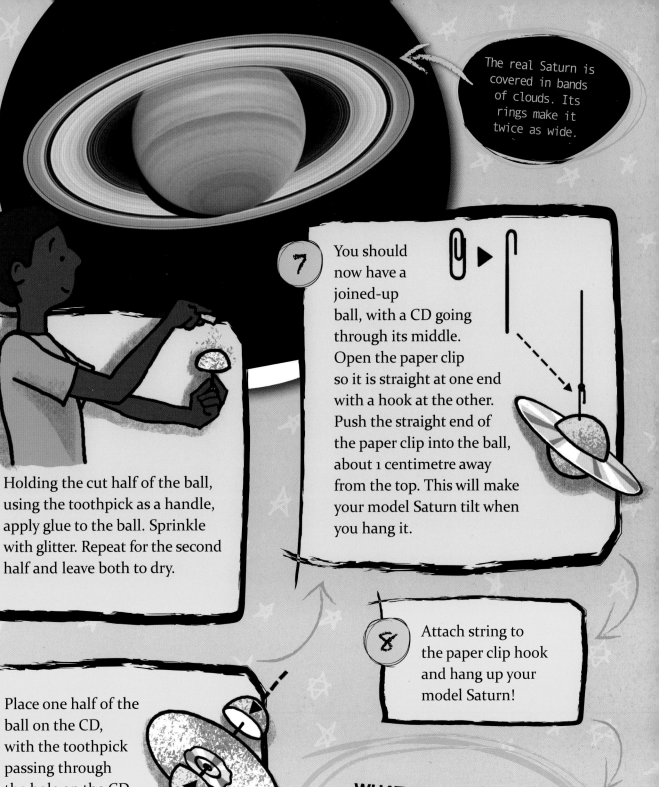

The real Saturn is covered in bands of clouds. Its rings make it twice as wide.

7 You should now have a joined-up ball, with a CD going through its middle. Open the paper clip so it is straight at one end with a hook at the other. Push the straight end of the paper clip into the ball, about 1 centimetre away from the top. This will make your model Saturn tilt when you hang it.

5 Holding the cut half of the ball, using the toothpick as a handle, apply glue to the ball. Sprinkle with glitter. Repeat for the second half and leave both to dry.

8 Attach string to the paper clip hook and hang up your model Saturn!

6 Place one half of the ball on the CD, with the toothpick passing through the hole on the CD. Place the other half of the ball on the other side of the CD. Push both halves of the ball onto the toothpick.

...WHAT DID YOU LEARN?

Does your CD Saturn look the same however you look at it? As Saturn and Earth move, our view of the rings changes. Sometimes they appear very wide, but at other times they are almost impossible to see.

PLUTO AND THE DWARFS

When it was discovered in 1930, Pluto became the ninth and most distant planet of the Solar System.

In 2006, astronomers decided that Pluto was too unusual to be called a normal planet. Pluto has since become known as a dwarf planet, and there are many other dwarf planets in the Solar System. Dwarf planets are different from normal planets because they are small and their path around the Sun is not always clear of other bodies. Astronomers think there may be hundreds of other dwarf planets still to find.

Little worlds

Pluto is a very cold and icy place. Its orbit takes it so far from the Sun that the temperature on its surface can drop to -230 degrees Celsius. Pluto is so cold that its atmosphere can freeze. The largest known dwarf planet is called Eris. It is even further from the Sun than Pluto.

Pluto has three moons, Charon and tiny Nix and Hydra. This is an imaginary view of Pluto from the surface of Nix.

Let's go there

In January 2006, NASA launched a spacecraft on a long journey to Pluto. The mission is called *New Horizons*. After a 5-billion-kilometre journey, the spacecraft will reach Pluto in 2015. *New Horizons* will send back the first ever close-up images of Pluto. It will also study other icy objects and perhaps find new dwarf planets.

New Horizons probe

From Earth, Pluto is too far away to see without a very large telescope. Even then it appears as a fuzzy ball.

What's in a name?

Pluto was named after the Roman god of the underworld. Venetia Burney, an 11-year-old English girl, suggested the name to her grandfather in 1930, and he passed it on to astronomers at the Lowell Observatory. All the planets (apart from Earth) are named after ancient gods. Mercury was named after the messenger of the gods, Venus after the Roman goddess of love and Jupiter after the king of gods.

PLANETS AROUND OTHER STARS

Astronomers have discovered that other stars also have planets orbiting around them.

Our Sun is not the only star with a system of planets and moons. Planets that orbit other stars are called **exoplanets**. Astronomers have so far discovered more than 600 exoplanets around distant stars. There could be billions of exoplanets in our Galaxy alone.

This artist's view shows the atmosphere of a hot exoplanet burning off because it is very close to its star.

Super-Earths

Astronomers are using very powerful telescopes to find small Earth-like exoplanets. They have found many that are likely to be rocky worlds. These are called super-Earths because they are bigger than Earth and 5 to 10 times heavier.

Hot Jupiters

Many of the exoplanets found so far are giant gas planets, like Jupiter or Saturn. But while Jupiter and Saturn orbit far away from the Sun, most of these exoplanets are much closer to their star. It's like imagining Jupiter orbiting closer to the Sun than Mercury does! These giant gas exoplanets are sometimes called hot Jupiters.

Some exoplanet systems have two stars at the centre. The planets orbit them both.

Other star systems

Just like our Sun, many other stars also have planets going around them. Experts think perhaps a half of all stars have a planet system. An example of a exoplanet system is called Kepler-11. This star is 2000 light-years away from Earth and has at least six planets. Most of these planets are the size of Uranus and Neptune. Five of the planets in Kepler-11 orbit closer to their star than Mercury does around the Sun.

LIFE BEYOND EARTH

There is water under the surfaces of the moons of Jupiter. Could there also be life?

Hundreds of new planets have been found orbiting around other stars. These exciting discoveries make us wonder whether life-forms may also exist on other planets and moons in space.

Goldilocks planets

Astronomers are looking for exoplanets similar to Earth where life could exist. They need to be the right distance from the Sun. Just like Goldilock's porridge, the planet must not be too hot or too cold. The Earth-like exoplanets must be at the right temperature so that oceans of liquid water can exist. Life is more likely to start on a warm, wet planet.

Earth is the only place in the Solar System where liquid water exists on the surface.

Life as we know it

Earth's living things survive in some very harsh places. For example, we find life in dark oceans where sunlight never shines. Even in baking hot deserts simple life forms such as bacteria can still survive. These environments are not so different from conditions in dry valleys on Mars or deep oceans of Jupiter's moon Europa. For life to exist on another planet it will need liquid water, and chemical **elements** such as carbon.

The Milky Way

Lots of Earths?

There are 200 billion stars in our galaxy, the Milky Way, and billions of these stars are like the Sun. One out of five of the Sun-like stars could have Earth-like planets. This means there could be almost a billion Earth-like planets just in our galaxy. That's a lot of planets where life may have started!

PAPER-CUP SUNDIAL

People have used sundials since ancient times to tell the time of day. Sundials use the changing shadow cast by the Sun as it rises and sets.

TRY DOING THIS...

In this activity you can make your own simple sundial to tell the time of day.

You will need:

* Large paper cup with a lid that has a hole for a straw
* Stiff straw (not a bendy one)
* Watch or clock
* Sharp pencil
* Sticky tape
* Sand or stones
* A compass that points to North

1 Make a hole in the side of the cup using the pencil. Make sure it is about 5 centimetres down from the top of the cup. The hole should be wide enough for a straw to pass through it.

5 cm

2 Half fill the cup with stones or sand to weigh it down. Put the lid on the cup.

Shadow length

When the Sun is high overhead, the shadows are at their shortest. The shadows are much longer in the early morning or late afternoon.

5 Find a place outside where the sunlight falls most of the day. Use a compass to point the straw to the North. At 10 a.m. mark a line on the lid to show where the shadow of the straw falls.

3 Push the straight straw through the hole in the lid and also through the hole in the side of the cup. The straw should stick up about 5 centimetres above the lid.

6 Repeat this every hour until 4 p.m. So you should have marked all the positions the shadow of the straw moved through each hour from 10 a.m. to 4 p.m., and written down the hours on the lid. The next sunny day, go back to the same place and read the time with your sundial.

4 Tape the other end of the straw onto the cup. Now you are ready to use your sundial.

...WHAT DID YOU LEARN?

The shadows move on the sundial because the Sun appears to move across the sky. But the Sun isn't really moving. It appears to move because the Earth is spinning around every 24 hours.

The Sun is always shining somewhere on Earth, even when it is night where you are.

Jewel box of stars

The night sky is a beautiful sight. Its stars sparkle and glitter like diamonds in a box of jewels.

Now you will learn all about the stars. Are all stars the same? What are they made of? How can there be stardust in our bodies? What type of star is the Sun? Will the stars shine forever, or will they burn out and die? Discover amazing answers to these questions and many more.

Blue and red stars

Stars don't all have the same colour. They can be blue, red, orange or yellow. Stars have different colours because their surfaces have different temperatures. Blue stars are the hottest and red stars are coolest.

Betelgeuse and Rigel are stars in the **constellation** Orion. Betelgeuse is orange, and Rigel is blue. Rigel has a surface temperature of 20,000 degrees Celsius – that's three times hotter than Betelgeuse.

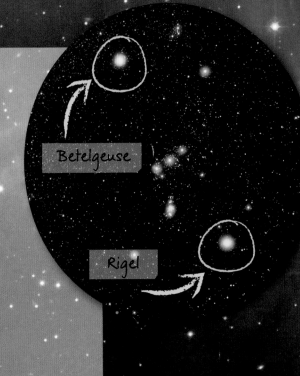

Betelgeuse

Rigel

A total of 6000 stars are bright enough to see without a telescope.

Bright ones and faint ones

Some stars are bright while others look faint. Stars can be brighter because they are more powerful. They put out more light energy, just like a giant floodlight in a sports stadium gives out much more light than a small torch. Some stars look dimmer because they are so far away.

The giant Sun

Why does the Sun look so big? The Sun is the star in our Solar System. It appears as a very large light in the sky, but it is about the same size as most of the other stars you see at night. It looks bigger because it is much closer to us than other stars.

The Sun is 150 million kilometres from the Earth.

Light-years away

Distances in space are unimaginably huge, so astronomers use a measurement called a light-year. One light-year is the distance that light travels in one year. Light moves very fast. It takes eight minutes to reach Earth from the Sun. However, it takes four years to arrive from our next nearest star – so scientists say that it is four light-years away. Rigel is 860 light-years from Earth.

WHERE STARS ARE BORN

One new star is born somewhere in our galaxy every year inside giant clouds of dust and gas.

The birthplace of a star is a **nebula,** a swirling cloud of hydrogen gas and specks of dust. Nebulae can have different shapes, and some glow with beautiful red, green and blue colours.

Squeezed by gravity

Gravity is the force that attracts one object to another. Inside a nebula gravity pulls the gas and dust together, squeezing it into a tight clump of matter. The clump gets hotter and hotter as the gas is pulled together. After millions of years, gravity has pressed the gas at the centre, or **core**, so much that it is 15 million degrees Celsius. The clump is now a newborn star. It is a fierce ball of hot glowing gases.

The new star shines at the heart of a swirling cloud of gas and dust.

Making planets

Unused gas and dust swirls around the new star, like a giant disc. It starts to clump into small rocks. These rocks crash together to make bigger and bigger bodies. They then trap gases around them, and finally we have planets with atmospheres, forming a solar system.

Rocks and planets form from the material left over when a star is born.

Star shine

Gravity packs the hydrogen in the star's core very tightly. The hydrogen is in tiny units called atoms. Because the atoms are so hot they move around very fast and smash into each other. Several hydrogen atoms join – or fuse – together to make a new gas called helium. This process, called **nuclear fusion**, releases huge amounts of heat and light, making the star shine.

WHY TWINKLE, TWINKLE LITTLE STAR?

You've probably sung the famous rhyme about a star that twinkles at night, but have you ever wondered why stars twinkle?

TRY DOING THIS...

Here is a simple activity to help you find out what makes the stars twinkle.

You will need:

* Sheet of aluminium foil
* Large piece of cardboard
* Torch
* Scissors
* Glass bowl
* Water

1 Cut six little star shapes out of the aluminium foil. Stars about 2 cm across will do fine.

← 2 cm →

2 Place the stars on the cardboard so that they will all be covered by the glass bowl.

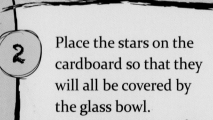

3 Fill about two thirds of the glass bowl with water and place it on top of the stars.

Bending light

When we look at stars, their light travels through the Earth's atmosphere before reaching our eyes. Winds make the air in the atmosphere move around. The shifting air causes the light from the stars to bend.

4 Darken the room by drawing the curtains and turning off the lights. Shine the torch from the top of the bowl and look at the stars at the bottom.

The light from stars twinkles as it passes through the Earth's atmosphere.

5 Now tap the side of the bowl to make the water ripple and look down at the stars from the top. Watch how the light from the stars appears to shimmer and twinkle!

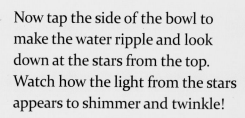

...WHAT DID YOU LEARN?

The moving water in the bowl is making the torch light bend as it travels to the bottom and reflects back off the aluminium stars. The bent path followed by the light makes the stars appear to move, or twinkle.

LIFE-STORY OF THE SUN

The stars we see in the night sky will not shine forever. At some point all stars will run out of fuel.

Stars are born, they burn for a time and then they die. The life cycle of a star takes billions of years. The Sun was born in a nebula about 5 billion years ago. Today, life on Earth thrives because of the warmth and light provided by the Sun. But things will be very different in our Solar System billions of years from now.

White dwarf

Big fluffy giant

The Sun's core has enough hydrogen to keep shining for another 5 billion years. Then it will swell up into a huge star called a **red giant**. After 100 million years as a red giant star, the Sun will then fall apart!

What will happen to the Earth?

As a red giant, the Sun will be 200 times bigger and 3000 times brighter than it is now. It will be so hot on our planet that the oceans will boil away. Even the rocky land will melt! But don't worry, this won't happen for another 5 billion years.

When the Sun becomes a red giant the Earth will be doomed!

Dying Sun

Earth

The final act

When the Sun has no fuel left its outer layers will be puffed out in giant shells called a **planetary nebula**. All that will be left behind will be the very hot and tightly packed core of the Sun, an object called a **white dwarf** star. The Sun will end its life as a white dwarf, gradually cooling over millions of years.

The Helix neb...
form...

REALLY MASSIVE STARS

There are incredibly powerful stars in the Universe that make our Sun look very small.

Our Sun has enough energy to shine for 10 billion years in total. Stars much heavier than the Sun shine more brightly. These massive stars use up their fuel supply of gases quicker than the Sun. A star that is born 20 times heavier than the Sun will shine 10,000 times brighter. But this star will only last for a few million years.

A doomed massive star expecting to explode in a supernova.

Making new atoms

We know the Sun turns hydrogen into helium in its hot core. But the centres of the biggest stars get much hotter, and the atoms are squeezed together to make atoms of heavier elements, such as carbon, oxygen, silicon and even iron.

Rigel

The Sun

Big and bigger

Some stars, such as Rigel, are so massive that
they are born 50 or 100 times heavier than the
Sun. The life story of a star depends on how
heavy it was when it was first formed. Really
massive stars have shorter and more violent
lives than our Sun.

The Crab Nebula
is the remains
of a supernova.
Chinese astronomers
saw the explosion
1000 years ago.

Giant explosion

When the biggest stars run out of fuel they
die in an explosion. As the huge star gets old,
it swells into a supergiant star. Gravity then
crushes the vast star into a core of iron.
As it collapses, the massive star dies in a bright
supernova explosion, which blows
the outer layers into space.

SUPERNOVA BLAST WAVE

When a massive star dies in a supernova explosion, a shock wave blasts away almost all of the gas layers of the star into space.

TRY DOING THIS...

In this activity we will use balls to explore how a blast wave can push out the layers of a star.

You will need:

✳ A ping pong (table tennis) ball
✳ A tennis ball
✳ A hard floor (not carpet or grass)

1 Hold the two balls together so that the ping pong ball is touching the top of the tennis ball. You can use two hands to do this.

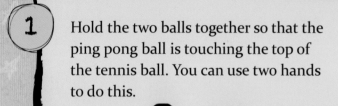

2 Think of the smaller ball as the outer layers of a massive star and the tennis ball as the star's heavy iron core.

1m

3 Hold the balls about 1 metre above the hard surface. Now let both balls drop down at the same time so the tennis ball hits the ground first, with the ping pong ball falling just above it.

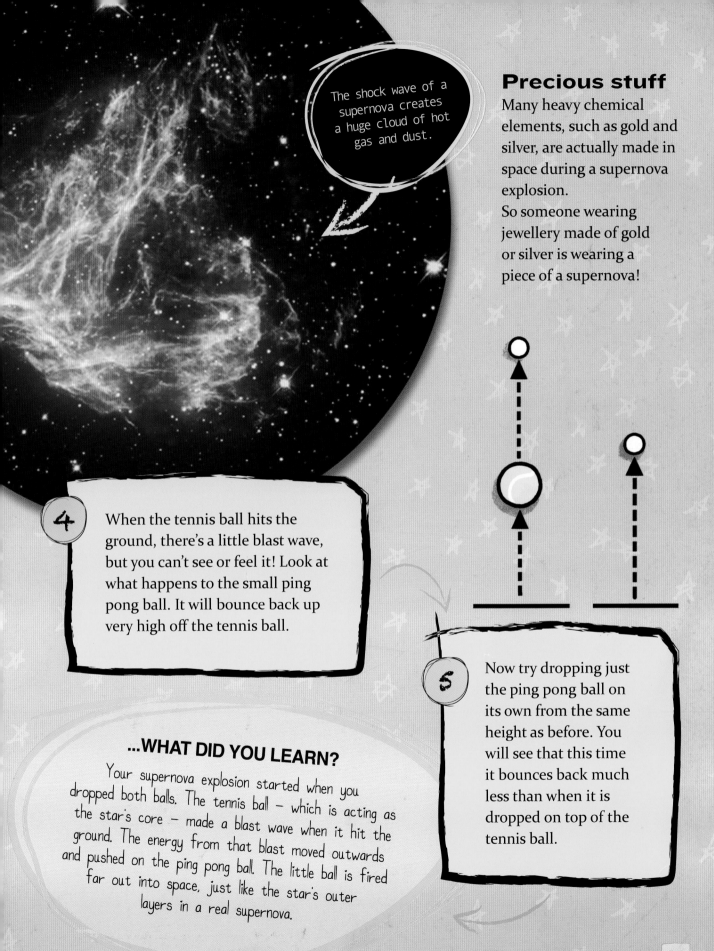

The shock wave of a supernova creates a huge cloud of hot gas and dust.

Precious stuff

Many heavy chemical elements, such as gold and silver, are actually made in space during a supernova explosion.

So someone wearing jewellery made of gold or silver is wearing a piece of a supernova!

4 When the tennis ball hits the ground, there's a little blast wave, but you can't see or feel it! Look at what happens to the small ping pong ball. It will bounce back up very high off the tennis ball.

5 Now try dropping just the ping pong ball on its own from the same height as before. You will see that this time it bounces back much less than when it is dropped on top of the tennis ball.

...WHAT DID YOU LEARN?

Your supernova explosion started when you dropped both balls. The tennis ball – which is acting as the star's core – made a blast wave when it hit the ground. The energy from that blast moved outwards and pushed on the ping pong ball. The little ball is fired far out into space, just like the star's outer layers in a real supernova.

WE ARE ALL MADE OF STARDUST

There is an amazing link between our lives on Earth and the lives and deaths of stars.

Many chemical elements are needed to make up the human body. We breathe in oxygen and have carbon in our cells, calcium in our bones and iron in the blood. Where did this stuff come from? The elements in our body were made inside stars!

Making the stuff of life

The elements needed for life are made by nuclear fusion inside stars. At the moment, the Sun is turning hydrogen into helium. As the Sun gets even hotter, the helium will be made into carbon. Massive stars can make many other elements.

A supernova blasts gas and dust into space, where it eventually forms a new star.

Making planets

Chemical elements pushed into space from a dying star became part of the nebula that made our Solar System. The planets were made from the carbon, silicon and iron dust that came from older stars far away. Some of that stardust has ended up in us!

Stardust clumps together to form new matter.

Spreading the elements

Thankfully for us the chemical elements that are made inside stars don't just stay locked in the stars forever. As a star gets older and runs out of energy, it starts to shed its outer layers of gas. When the Sun is a red giant star it will puff out lots of layers that have helium and carbon in them. In much heavier stars, the powerful supernova explosion pushes away the silicon, oxygen and iron that was made inside the star and scatters it into space.

EXPLODING STARS

Dying stars make some of the biggest explosions in the Universe, and young stars experience raging storms.

During its life – and death – a star puts out huge amounts of energy. Sometimes this energy is released all at once in powerful explosions. Some explosions have so much energy that they can even be seen in other galaxies very far away from us. The bursts can even destroy the star itself. Let us take a closer look at the explosions made by stars.

The Earth could fit inside this bubble of gas blasting from the Sun 25 times over.

Bubbling Sun

Sometimes there are storms on the Sun. Super-hot bubbles explode from the surface making clouds of electrified gas. If a bubble hits Earth it can damage space satellites in orbit and even cause power cuts on the surface. A giant solar storm caused a massive power cut in North America and Canada in 1989.

Rocking the Universe

When stars 100 times heavier than the Sun die, they produce the most powerful explosions of all. Known as a **hypernova**, one of these incredible blasts packs more power than 10,000 normal supernovae put together! Hypernovae rock the Universe!

As the gas is blasted out from a supernova, it becomes hotter than the surface of the Sun.

Supernova

A supernova is one of the most powerful events in the Universe. We saw earlier how stars much heavier than the Sun end their lives in awesome blasts that rip them apart. The blast from a supernova will throw matter into space at an amazing speed of 40,000 kilometres per second. A supernova explosion is 10 billion times as bright as the Sun. It can even outshine the galaxy it is in.

COUNTING THE STARS

There are almost 200 billion stars in our Galaxy, but how many can you see with just your eyes?

You will need:

* Large piece of stiff cardboard (21 x 21 sq. cm)
* Ruler
* Pencil
* Scissors
* Long length of strong string
* Notebook

21 cm
1.5 cm
18 cm

1 First make your viewing frame. Use the ruler and pencil to draw a 1.5 cm border along each side of the card. Cut along the border and remove the piece in the middle.

Ask an adult to help.

2 Make a hole in the middle of one border. Cut a length of string 80 cm long, and loop it through the hole. Tie the ends of the string into a knot.

Ask an adult to help.

3 Put the string around your neck and hold the frame away from you until the string is fully stretched. This will make sure that the viewer is the same distance from your eyes each time you use it.

Light pollution!

You should notice that the star counts made in dark locations, such as the countryside, are much higher than in a city. This is because light pollution from the street lamps and buildings in cities makes it harder for us to see the stars.

Where are all the rest?

From very dark places on clear nights you can see almost 2000 stars. The other billions of stars in our Milky Way Galaxy are too faint and far away for us to see them directly. Astronomers use powerful telescopes to view, and study, many more stars.

Some stars are brighter than others, and you need to look carefully to see them all.

 4 Go outside on a clear night. Hold up the viewer and count how many stars you can see inside the frame. Do this five times, with the viewer pointed towards a different part of the sky. Write the numbers in your notebook.

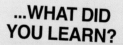

 5 Add up the five values that you wrote in your notebook and divide the total by five. That gives you the average number of stars you saw through your viewer.

...WHAT DID YOU LEARN?

The window in your frame is about 40 times smaller than the full stretch of the sky. Multiply your average number by 40 to get an estimate of the total number of stars we can see in the night sky. Try using your star viewer in different locations, such as the countryside and in a city.

GRAVEYARD OF STARS

When stars run out of energy and die, they leave behind a graveyard of very weird objects.

With no fuel left to keep the star shining, the force of gravity takes over and crushes what remains of the star. The type of object left in space will depend on how heavy the star was when it was first born. Here are three awesome types of dead star – **neutron stars**, white dwarfs and black holes.

A black hole is invisible, but its surroundings glow brightly.

Neutron star

Neutron stars

Stars that weigh 10 to 20 times more than the Sun end their lives as neutron stars. Neutron stars are made in supernova explosions. What was once a huge star is squeezed by gravity to a ball the size of a city. To make Earth as tightly packed as a neutron star it would have to be crushed to the size of a raindrop! Neutron stars can spin hundreds of times in a second.

Black holes

The heaviest of stars make the strangest objects in space when they die. Stars that weigh more than 20 times the Sun become mysterious black holes. After a supernova nothing can stop gravity from crushing the matter that is left. When you make something smaller by crushing it, its gravity becomes even stronger. A black hole crams the star's material into a tiny space. Its gravity is so strong that even light cannot escape from it – that is why it is black.

White dwarfs

At the end of its life, a lightweight star will be crushed inside its planetary nebula into an object called a white dwarf. A spoonful of white dwarf would weigh as much on Earth as an elephant!

RECYCLING IN SPACE

The life-story of a star keeps an amazing cosmic cycle turning as new stars form from dead ones.

Over billions of years chemical elements are recycled several times over. This process is very important in providing the material needed to make planets, oceans and life. Let's go around the cosmic cycle.

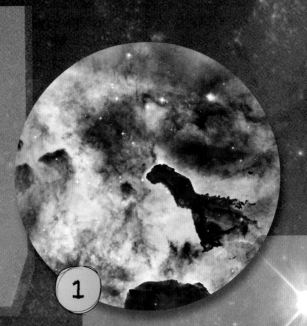

1

Clouds in space
We start the cycle with the giant cloud of gas from which stars are made. Lots of hydrogen and other elements are found in these star-making factories.

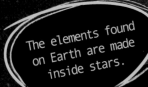

The elements found on Earth are made inside stars.

2

Star life
Once a star is born, it spends its life releasing the energy that makes it shine. The energy comes from nuclear fusion in its fiercely hot centre. During fusion, hydrogen, helium, carbon, oxygen, iron and other elements are made inside stars.

Spreading stardust

The chemical elements made inside stars are released into space as the stars get older. Red giant stars and supernova explosions spew enormous amounts of stardust into space. These hot gases shoot into space and spread slowly over vast distances.

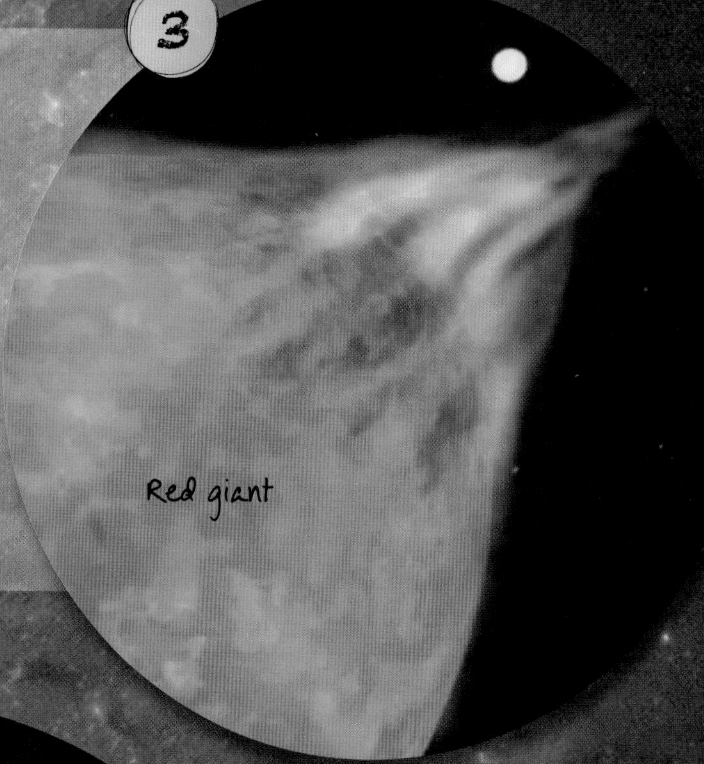

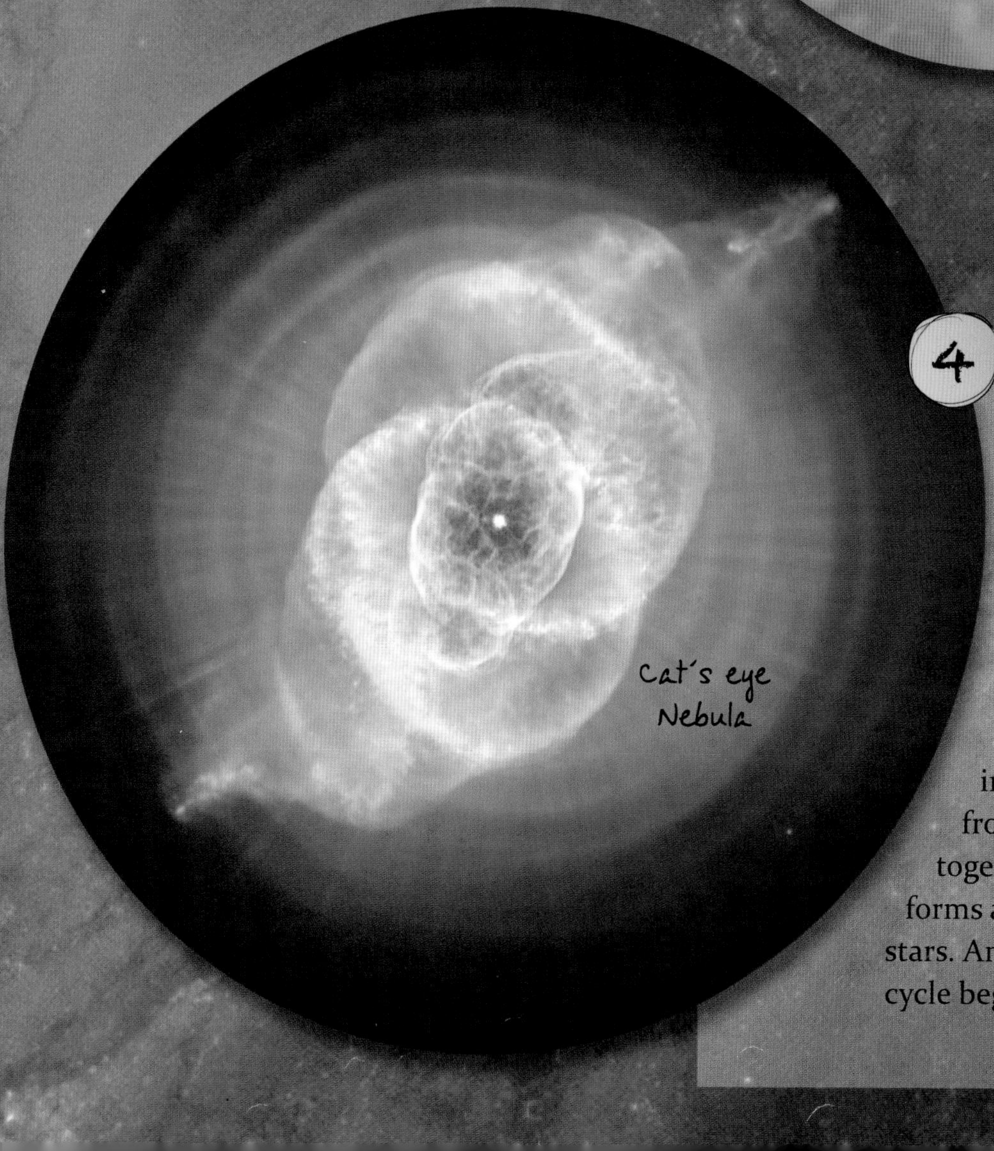

3

Red giant

4

Back into the clouds

After billions of years, the outer layers blasted out when a star dies will join other nebulae out in space. The clouds from several stars mix together until the stardust forms a new generation of stars. And the whole cosmic cycle begins again!

Cat's eye Nebula

INVENT A CONSTELLATION

Constellations are imaginary patterns in the sky. They are made up of lines between the stars. It's like playing dot-to-dot with the night sky!

TRY DOING THIS...

In this activity you get to make up your own constellation and write a myth about it!

You will need:

* Large sheet of black card or thick paper
* Packet of silver star stickers
* White crayon
* Ruler
* Pencil and notebook

Constellations are a way of organising the random pattern made by stars.

1 Place the black paper on a flat surface.

2 With your eyes closed, stick 12 to 16 silver star stickers on the black paper. Try to spread out the stars a little as you place them – don't bunch them close together.

Sailing by the stars

Constellations have had an important role in human history. They have been used by ancient civilizations to tell myths and stories. Sailors used constellations to navigate across the seas. There are 88 constellations in the sky, including famous ones such as Orion (the Hunter), Scorpio (the Scorpion), Taurus (the Bull) and Cygnus (the Swan).

Scorpio

Taurus

3 Now open your eyes and look at the stars. Imagine being an ancient astronomer. Think of a pattern you could make with lines joining the stars. Perhaps you can make up an animal shape.

4 Once you've worked out a pattern, use the white crayon and ruler to draw straight lines between the stars. Stand back and look at your new constellation!

5 Now your constellation needs a name and a myth or story about it. When and where does your story take place? What type of beast or character is it? Perhaps it has special powers. Maybe there's a big battle with another constellation!

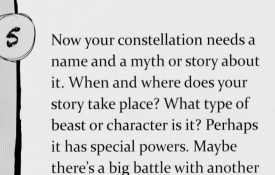

...WHAT DID YOU LEARN?

All constellations are just made up — even the ones used by astronomers. There are as many possible patterns in the sky as there are stars. The patterns people often see are everyday things, such as animals or people, but a constellation could be anything.

LET THERE BE LIGHT

We live in very exciting times for exploring space and making amazing discoveries about the Universe.

Scientists use remarkably powerful telescopes to study distant galaxies and stars. We also launch spacecraft from Earth to orbit and even land on the planets and moons in our Solar System. Now we will learn about some of the biggest telescopes used to study the Universe and fly along with spacecraft missions that explore the Solar System. We also look at some new ways scientists are making exciting discoveries in space.

Fuel tank

Space shuttle

Launch tower

Hot gases from engines push the spacecraft upward.

Can't we just go there?

The stars and galaxies are unimaginably vast distances away from us. Even light, which travels at 300,000 kilometres a second, takes millions of years to reach us from some objects in the huge Universe. Our spacecraft are far too slow to visit these places. However, spacecraft can be flown to planets and moons in our Solar System because they are much closer than the stars.

Light from space

To learn about planets, stars and galaxies, astronomers have to collect the light coming from them. Astronomers use powerful telescopes to make images of the objects, which they then examine in detail. Sometimes the telescopes are launched into space and orbit around the Earth.

Telescopes make it possible to see this galaxy in great detail.

Invisible light

We see things using the light that enters our eyes. But the light we see with our eyes is just one type of light. There are many other forms that are invisible to us. Using special equipment we can detect low-energy light such as **infrared** and radio waves. There are also telescopes that can pick up high-energy rays, such as ultraviolet light, **X-rays** and **gamma rays**.

Radio telescope

LIGHT BUCKETS

Since the telescope was invented more than 400 years ago, larger and larger machines have been built to study the Universe.

You can think of a telescope as a large bucket that collects light! Telescopes are instruments used by astronomers to make distant objects appear bigger and faraway things seem closer. Telescopes allow us to see incredible things in space that cannot be seen with human eyes alone.

This observatory in Chile is 3000 metres up a mountain where there is a clear view of the sky.

How do telescopes work?

Telescopes use mirrors or **lenses** to see distant objects. Bigger telescopes collect more light from a star, making the image a lot clearer. Most telescopes have two main pieces. They have a large mirror that collects light and reflects it into a sharp point called a focus. The second part is an eyepiece that makes the focused light appear larger.

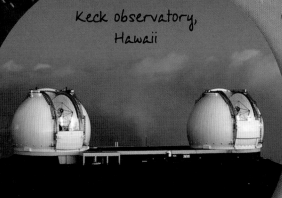
Keck observatory, Hawaii

Great observatories

Today's astronomers use giant telescopes that have mirrors 10 metres wide. The telescopes are kept inside huge domes called observatories. Many observatories are perched on high mountains, well away from the glare of lights in cities. These observatories also use other scientific equipment and powerful computers to make the telescopes work.

How powerful are the telescopes?

The best modern observatories have remarkable power. They can turn very faint objects in space into sharp, detailed pictures. The giant Keck telescopes in Hawaii are so powerful they could see the flame of a normal candle placed as far away as the Moon! The 8-metre wide VLT telescope in Chile allows us to see objects four billion times fainter than those we can see with our eyes alone.

MAKE A RAINBOW

We have learnt that astronomers study many different types of light. Even the visible white light we see with our eyes is made up of many colours.

You will need:

- ✳ A wide glass bowl
- ✳ Water
- ✳ White card
- ✳ A small hand mirror
- ✳ Sticky tack
- ✳ Sunshine

TRY DOING THIS...

In this activity you can make your own rainbow to see how the white light in sunshine can be split into red, orange, yellow, green, blue, indigo and violet.

1 Place the glass bowl on a table in a sunny position.

2 Put the hand mirror in the bowl, making sure it leans at a small angle against the side of the bowl. Keep the mirror in place by using sticky tack on the back of the mirror.

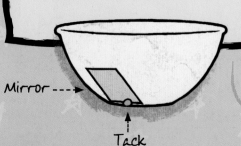

Mirror ---->

Tack

3 Fill the glass bowl with water until the whole of the mirror is covered. Turn the bowl to keep the mirror directly in the sunlight.

A rainbow is made by white light splitting when it shines through rain drops.

Invisible light

If you had a special camera, you could see the invisible light in a rainbow. Just beyond the red side of a rainbow there is infrared (below red) light. Beyond the violet light there are ultraviolet (above violet) rays.

4 Now hold the white card next to the bowl on the opposite side from the mirror. Move the card around until you can see the reflection of sunlight from the mirror on the card.

5 You should see a small image on the card that looks like part of a rainbow!

...WHAT DID YOU LEARN?

The white sunlight reflects off the mirror in the bowl, and as it passes up through the water the light is bent. This makes the white light split up into the colours of the rainbow. Something similar happens when the Sun comes out during rain. The sunlight strikes droplets of rain and is broken up into a set of colours. We see this as a rainbow arching across the sky.

TELESCOPES IN SPACE

Some telescopes are launched into space on board rockets and placed into orbit around the Earth.

Different types of space telescope study different types of light. Telescopes that can see X-rays and ultraviolet light are used to study the hottest stars, such as exploding supernovae. Infrared-sensing telescopes reveal how stars are born out of cool clouds of gas. Earth's atmosphere blurs the light shining through it, so putting a telescope in space above the atmosphere means we can see objects much more clearly.

Light comes in here

Chandra X-ray Observatory

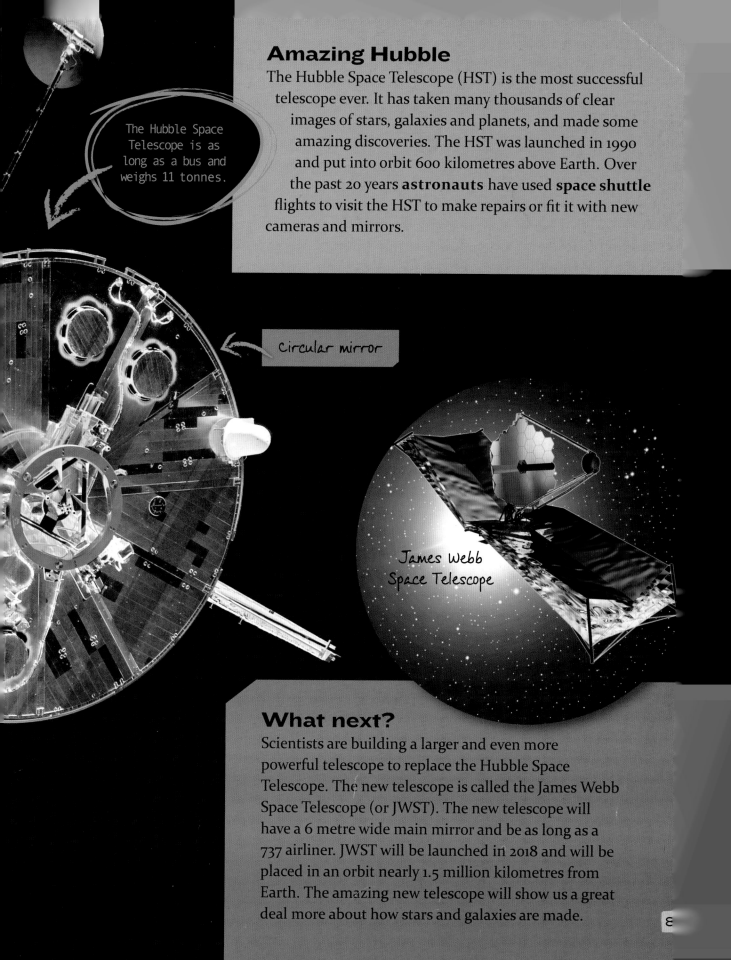

Amazing Hubble

The Hubble Space Telescope (HST) is the most successful telescope ever. It has taken many thousands of clear images of stars, galaxies and planets, and made some amazing discoveries. The HST was launched in 1990 and put into orbit 600 kilometres above Earth. Over the past 20 years **astronauts** have used **space shuttle** flights to visit the HST to make repairs or fit it with new cameras and mirrors.

The Hubble Space Telescope is as long as a bus and weighs 11 tonnes.

Circular mirror

James Webb Space Telescope

What next?

Scientists are building a larger and even more powerful telescope to replace the Hubble Space Telescope. The new telescope is called the James Webb Space Telescope (or JWST). The new telescope will have a 6 metre wide main mirror and be as long as a 737 airliner. JWST will be launched in 2018 and will be placed in an orbit nearly 1.5 million kilometres from Earth. The amazing new telescope will show us a great deal more about how stars and galaxies are made.

SPACE STATIONS

Space stations are large spacecraft that allow astronauts to live and work in space for long periods of time.

The International Space Station (ISS) is the largest object ever built in space. It is so big that more than 40 rockets and space shuttle flights were needed to carry all the parts into space. The ISS was built by many countries working together. It is almost the size of a football pitch and can even be seen in the night sky from Earth! There are several different rooms called modules where astronauts live, work and sleep.

cooling panels

Valery Polyakov looks out of the window of *Mir*, the Russian space station where he lived.

Living in space

There is no gravity inside a space station, so the astronauts float. This means they don't use their muscles much. The astronauts' bodies can become weak after a long time in space, and so the crew do lots of exercise every day. Russian Valery Polyakov spent 438 days living in space – longer than anyone else. He orbited Earth 7075 times and travelled 300 million kilometres!

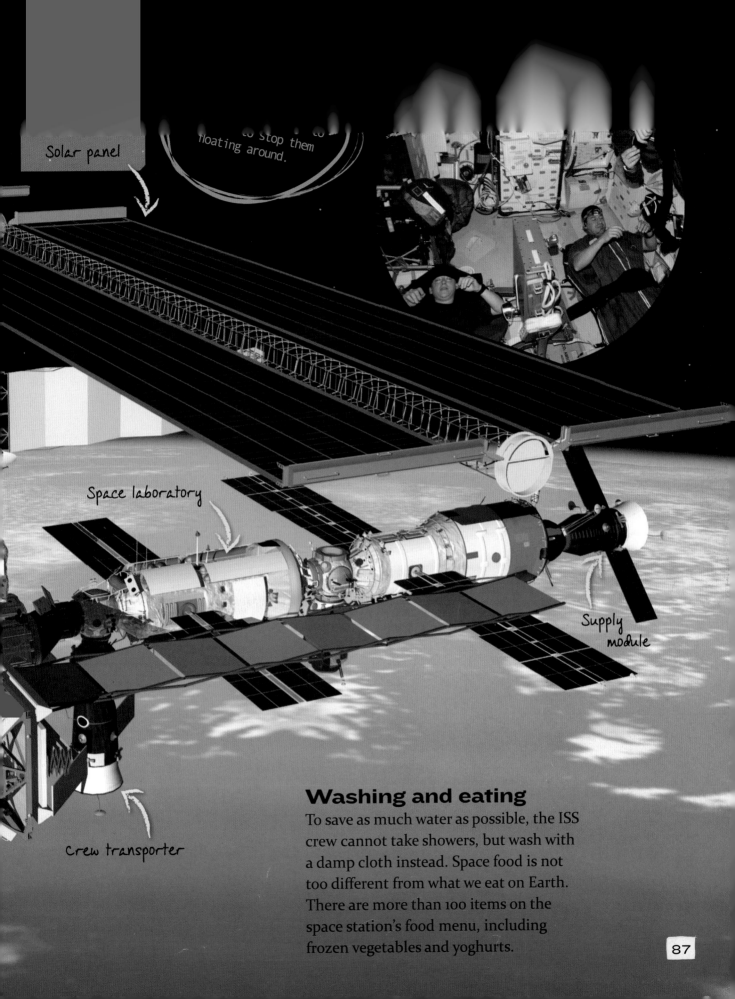

Solar panel

to stop them
floating around.

Space laboratory

Supply
module

Crew transporter

Washing and eating

To save as much water as possible, the ISS
crew cannot take showers, but wash with
a damp cloth instead. Space food is not
too different from what we eat on Earth.
There are more than 100 items on the
space station's food menu, including
frozen vegetables and yoghurts.

BALLOON ROCKET

Rockets blasting off from Earth are an amazing sight. They can weigh hundreds of tonnes at liftoff, but hot gases pushed out at very high speeds have enough power to lift the rocket off the ground.

TRY DOING THIS...

Rockets normally burn a fuel made of liquid hydrogen and liquid oxygen. In this activity you can explore how a rocket works using air as the fuel!

You will need:

* ✴ About 5 metres of strong string
* ✴ A few plastic straws (not bendy ones)
* ✴ Sticky tape
* ✴ Some balloons with a mixture of long and rounded shapes

1 Tie one end of the string to a fixture in the room such as a chair or door handle.

2 Thread the other end of the string through the straw and pull it tight. Tie the loose end of the string to another fixed object, keeping it tight. Move the straw to the middle of the string.

3 Cut two pieces of sticky tape. Now blow up the balloon and pinch the end so that the air does not come out. Tape the balloon under the straw using the tape. You might need some help with the tape while you hold the balloon.

Rockets travel at 28,000 kilometres per hour to escape Earth's gravity.

4 You're now ready for launch. Let go of the balloon and watch it fly across the room.

...WHAT DID YOU LEARN?

Like all rockets, your balloon rocket works because of thrust. Thrust is the force that moves the rocket. The air pushing out from the balloon gives thrust to move your rocket. The burning fuel in real rockets blasts hot gases down towards the ground. The hot blast pushes the rocket upwards.

Further experiments

Try to experiment with different shapes of balloon, filling the balloon with more or less air, and changing the size of the straw by cutting it in half or quarter. See how the speed and distance travelled by the balloon changes.

MISSIONS TO THE PLANETS

Over the past 50 years we have made fantastic new discoveries about planets by sending spacecraft to explore the Solar System.

Spacecraft have been sent to every planet in the Solar System. We've even landed probes on the surfaces of Venus, Mars and Saturn's moon Titan, and visited some asteroids and comets. None of these missions carried any astronauts. The Moon is the only place beyond Earth that has been visited by humans. Between July 1969 and December 1972, twelve astronauts walked on the Moon. No one has been back to the Moon since.

Beyond the Solar System

Some spacecraft have actually left the Solar System. The *Voyager 1* probe was launched in 1977 and is now over 100 times farther from the Sun than Earth is. The *Pioneer 11* spacecraft, launched in 1975, is now more than 11 billion kilometres away from Earth. This probe is carrying drawings of humans. Who knows, maybe one day it will be found by an alien civilisation!

The Huygens lander parachuted to the surface of Titan – and found lakes full of oil!

Keeping a close eye on Mars

More spacecraft missions have been sent to Mars than to any other planet. Using orbiters and **landers**, astronomers have learnt a great deal about the atmosphere and surface of Mars, and have even found tiny amounts of water ice. Since 2004 **rovers** have also been driving around on the surface of Mars. Like radio-controlled cars, the rovers get instructions from Earth telling them to move to new locations and examine rocks and soil.

Camera arm

Radio dish

Solar panel

This Mars rover is called *Opportunity*. Its job is to study the surface of Mars.

WHERE TO NEXT?

Scientists are planning to launch even more amazing spacecraft. In the future, faster rockets and clever robots will let us explore more of the Solar System.

A crewed mission to another planet, such as Mars, would be difficult. Spacecraft carrying fuel, water and building materials would be sent first. Only then could a crew set off. It takes nearly seven months to fly there. There is no oxygen on Mars so the base would need machines to recycle air and water. Vegetables could be grown in greenhouses. The crew would live underground to stay safe from dangerous radiation.

Training on the Moon

Back to the Moon

Many scientists think that returning to the Moon is an important way to train for a Mars mission. The Moon and Mars are similar. Both have gravity that is weaker than that on Earth. There is no air to breathe on the Moon, so it's a good place to learn how to survive by purifying water for drinking and turning into rocket fuel. It is also easier to test technologies on the Moon since it is just a three-day rocket ride away.

Drilling on icy moons

Scientists plan to drop landers on icy moons of Jupiter and Saturn. They want to drill through their surfaces to reach huge oceans of water that are thought to lie beneath. They may find simple life forms that survive in the deep, dark alien oceans.

It can get very cold on Mars and the atmosphere is very thin. Without a spacesuit, the astronaut's blood would freeze.

SUPER HEARING

Spacecraft send back very weak radio signals to Earth, and it can be difficult to pick up the tiny whispers from the distant spacecraft.

TRY DOING THIS...

In this simple activity you can make your own sound detector and explore how tiny signals increase in power using wide antennae.

You will need:

* A large (40 x 60 centimetres) piece of thin card
* Sticky tape
* A friend to help make sounds

1 Roll the card into the shape of a cone. Leave a 2 centimetre hole at the pointed end and make the large end of the cone as wide as possible.

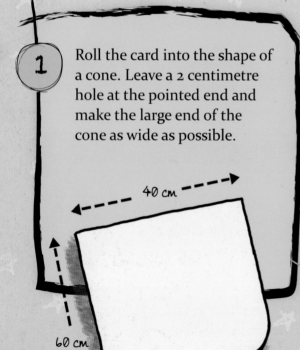

40 cm

60 cm

2 Use the sticky tape to secure the edge of the card so that the cone does not open up.

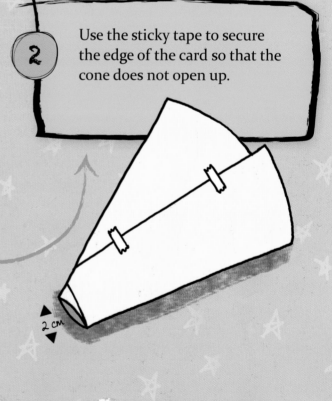

2 cm

Dish detectors

Spacecraft travel millions or even billions of kilometres from Earth. Very large dish-shaped receivers called **antennae** are pointed at the sky to detect the weak signals.

The dish collects weak radio signals and directs them to a detection antenna in the centre.

3 Go outside and listen to some sounds, first with just your ears and then by placing the cone against your ear. Get a friend to stand many metres away and make very weak sounds, like gently tapping a couple of pebbles together.

Ask a friend to help.

click click

4 Notice how much easier it is to hear the tapping sound with your cone. See how far away your friend can walk while you can still hear the sound. Now try to listen without the cone.

...WHAT DID YOU LEARN?

The shape of the cone helps to move the sound waves to a point near your ear. Because the radio signals from spacecraft are so weak, the antennae have to be very large, like using a huge cone! The largest antennae are 70 metres across.

SAILING TO THE STARS

Today's spacecraft take several years to reach the planets. To travel to stars we will need new, much faster spaceships.

The stars are very far away. The nearest star to the Sun, called Proxima Centauri, is almost 100,000 times farther away than the outer planet Neptune. Using current rocket engines it would take more than 20,000 years to reach Proxima Centauri!

Solar sails

A new way of getting spacecraft to move much faster in space is to use solar sails. A solar sail is made of a huge mirror-like surface that is pushed along by light. The force is produced by sunlight reflecting off the shiny side of the sail. Gradually, as more and more sunlight hits the sail, the spacecraft rises to super-high speeds.

In the future starships might be powered by enormous solar sails built in space.

A space colony, like this artist's impression, would be home to people colonizing a planet.

Laser powered

A laser can be focussed into a very tiny beam of light packed with energy. One day we might be able to launch small but fast spacecraft that are pushed along by lasers shining onto solar sails.

Colonies on the move

Even a large laser-powered solar sail doing 1000 kilometres per second would take 1300 years to reach the nearest star. If humans are to travel between stars we will have to build space colonies with farmers, doctors and teachers on board. None of the people leaving Earth will reach the final destination, but their descendants will.

So you want to be an astronaut?

You don't need superhero powers to become an astronaut. But you will need to work very hard if your dream is to fly into space.

The journey to becoming an astronaut starts very early. You have to study hard at school and do well in subjects like maths and science. If you want to be a commander of a spacecraft then you'll have to train to become a top pilot who can fly fast jet aircraft.

Spacewalk training

Cargo bay

Spacewalking

Astronauts learn to spacewalk – or move around outside the spacecraft. They train for this in huge swimming pools, where they float in the same way as in space.

Specialist at work

Astronaut jobs

The commander is the pilot of the spacecraft and leads the whole mission. There are also mission specialists who carry out experiments in space or go on spacewalks to mend the spacecraft.

Crowded crew

Living together

Astronauts have to live and work in very small modules on spacecraft. You will need to enjoy working in a team and be prepared to help others. One thing is for sure – the view from your office in space will be fantastic!

SLEEP AND GROW

We have learnt that in space astronauts have to live and work in zero gravity. The force of gravity can affect your height, as this activity will demonstrate.

TRY DOING THIS...

In this activity you can explore how the pull of gravity can change your height in just one day!

You will need:
* A flat hard floor and wall to stand against
* Help of an adult
* A hardbacked book
* A pencil
* A measuring tape

1 Find a place in your home with a hard level floor and wall that you can stand against to have your height measured.

2 Ask an adult to help. Last thing at night, just before going to bed, stand upright against the wall and ask an adult to place the book on your head. Keep the book still and move away from the wall.

3 Ask an adult to help. Ask the adult to carefully mark the position of the bottom of the book using the pencil. Use the measuring tape to measure the distance from the floor to the pencil mark. This should be an accurate measure of your height at bedtime.

Growing strong
On Earth, gravity helps our bodies to make thick bones and strong muscles. In space without gravity the muscles and bones of the astronauts can become much weaker.

Weightless

When in orbit, astronauts have no weight – gravity does not pull them down, so they just float. It takes a bit of practice to get used to being weightless. Even astronauts feel a bit travel-sick when they first arrive in orbit.

This astronaut is floating in orbit. He moves using tiny rockets on his backpack.

5 Notice how you are about 1 centimetre taller when you wake up in the morning than you are last thing at night!

Ask an adult to help.

4 Now repeat the same measurement first thing in the morning when you wake up, making sure to stand in the same place. You need to measure the height again carefully, and even repeat the two measurements over a few days and nights.

WHAT WE LEARNED...

You are slightly taller in the morning than at night because of the force of gravity. During the day gravity pulls down on your spine. The bones in the spine are squeezed closer together. All this pushing can make you lose a little height during the day. At night, when you are lying flat, the bones spread out again so you stretch back to full height.

REALLY COOL STUFF ABOUT GALAXIES AND THE UNIVERSE

Galaxies and the Big Bang are important subjects. They lead to some amazing discoveries in space!

What's the biggest galaxy smash?

About 5 billion light-years away a cosmic pile-up has four galaxies colliding. Three of the galaxies are about the size of the Milky Way, while the fourth is three times as big! Stars are being thrown into space by this huge crash.

Could a black hole gobble up the Solar System?

Astronomers have found a massive black hole that weighs as much as 18 billion Suns. This monster lurks in the centre of a quasar. It is so big that it could swallow our Solar System whole!

Are there great walls in the Universe?

There are chains of galaxies hundreds of millions of light-years long. The largest known structure in the Universe is an enormous wall of galaxies that spreads across 200 million light-years. In total this gigantic wall has 300 times more matter than our entire Milky Way Galaxy.

What's pulling the Milky Way Galaxy?

The Milky Way, along with other galaxies, is being pulled by the gravity of a mysterious object called the Great Attractor. This is so enormous that the Milky Way is flying towards it at an amazing speed of 22 million kilometres per hour!

Can you hear bangs in space?

In films, explosions in space, such as stars blowing up, are given loud sound effects. The movie makers are making up the sound! The sounds we hear every day are actually waves in the air. When the moving air reaches our ear drums, we can hear the sound. There is no air in space. Without any air, there is no sound in space either.

Are we being blasted with rays from space?

Billions of tiny particles called cosmic rays are slamming into the Earth every second. Luckily for us, the Earth's atmosphere protects us from most of them.

Are there super-sized galaxies?

The largest galaxies are egg-shaped and are found in the centre of galaxy clusters. This central galaxy grows by gobbling up smaller galaxies. There is a giant galaxy 5.5 million light-years across in the centre of a galaxy cluster. This makes it 60 times larger than our own.

Where is the centre of the Universe?

There is no centre to the Universe! The whole Universe is expanding in all directions and pushing itself away from everything else.

Did the Universe start really hot?

Just one second after the Big Bang, the temperature of the Universe was 10 billion degrees Celsius. It has slowly cooled over the past 13 to 14 billion years and is now a freezing –270 degrees Celsius!

How big is the Universe?

Nobody knows the exact size of the Universe because we can't see its edge. Today we can see to a distance of nearly 13 billion light-years in all directions, so it is at least this size.

REALLY COOL STUFF ABOUT PLANETS

Every planet is a world of its own, with many remarkable features that are literally out of this world!

Do comets crash into the Sun?

The Sun is a massive object with very strong gravity. Sometimes comets swinging in from the outer parts of the solar system come too close to the Sun and get trapped by the enormous pull of the Sun's gravity. The comets can end up crashing into the Sun!

Can you walk on asteroids?

Asteroids are mostly very small and so their gravity is very weak. An astronaut standing on an asteroid would weigh very little. This makes taking steps on the asteroid very difficult and the astronaut would mostly float on the surface.

Is it raining diamonds on Neptune?

Neptune has a lot of methane gas in its huge atmosphere. Scientists think that the temperature and force of the gas inside Neptune is so high that the methane can turn into diamonds! Once the diamonds are made they would fall like raindrops toward the centre of the planet.

Did something from space kill the dinosaurs?

Some scientists think that most dinosaurs died when a huge asteroid struck Earth about 65 million years ago. The powerful crash made giant clouds of dust rise into the air and block out the sunlight for many months. The dust changed the climate and made the dinosaurs die out.

What are Solar flares?

Every now and then small patches on the Sun erupt in flashes, known as flares. These release huge amounts of energy. The largest solar flare can blast billions of tons of superhot gas into space. The amount of energy released in a single flare can be millions of times larger than that of a volcano exploding on Earth.

Why is Uranus on its side?

All planets spin vertically on their axes, apart from Uranus. This spins on its side, like a barrel rolling around the Sun! It could be that massive Earth-sized objects crashed into it billions of years ago and knocked it over!

Will Mars have a ring one day?

One of Mars' two moons is called Phobos. This moon is slowly moving towards the planet. In perhaps 10 million years from now, Phobos will get so close to Mars that the planet's gravity will break the small moon apart. When Phobos shatters the material will form a thin ring around Mars!

Why is there a big red spot on Jupiter?

A hurricane has been raging on Jupiter for more than 400 years! It is called the Great Red Spot because of the way it looks. Almost three Earths could fit side-by-side inside it.

Is Earth's Moon drifting away?

The distance between the Earth and its Moon has been measured carefully using lasers since astronauts visited the Moon in the

Is there acid rain on Venus?

Clouds on Venus are made of a very nasty acid called sulphuric acid. But Venus is so hot that acid rain never falls to the ground. It evaporates high above the surface.

REALLY COOL STUFF ABOUT STARS

We've learned how stars form, how they shine brightly and then die. But there are many more things to discover.

What are Sun quakes?

Earthquakes on our planet are very dangerous. The Sun also has quakes, with huge ripples in the upper layers. Just like those on Earth, quakes on the Sun tell us about what the Sun is made of.

How many stars are there in the Universe?

The best estimate is 20 thousand billion billion stars, or the number 2 followed by 22 zeros. That's almost as many stars as there are grains of dry sand on all the beaches on Earth!

Do ghostly particles come from the Sun?

When nuclear fusion happens inside the Sun, some of the energy is put out as mysterious particles called neutrinos. These tiny particles can pass right through matter, just like ghosts! Almost a trillion neutrinos will pass through your body while you read this sentence!

Are there diamonds in the sky?

The insides of some dead stars are made of carbon, the same stuff that makes diamonds. The largest known diamond is inside a white dwarf star 50 light-years away. The diamond is almost 4000 kilometres across!

Can stars crash?

Sometimes thousands of stars are tightly packed in a cluster. In the middle of these clusters stars can collide with enormous power. The wreckage that's left can be squeezed by gravity to make a new, much hotter star.

How fast does the Sun move?

All stars in space are not still. Our Sun and its family of planets are flying at almost 70,000 kilometres per hour towards the constellation of Lyra. The Milky Way Galaxy is spinning, and the Sun makes a giant trip around it every 225 million years.

Where do the stars go during the day?

Only the Sun is visible by day. The rest of the stars are still there but you can't see them because the blue sky is so bright.

What happens if I fall inside a black hole?

Your feet will feel a stronger pull of gravity than your head, so as you go into the black hole you will be stretched until you are as thin as spaghetti!

What is the largest star in the Universe?

The largest of all known stars is called VY Canis Majoris. This monster is so big that if you placed it at the centre of our Solar System, it would gobble up Mercury, Venus, Earth, Mars and Jupiter!

Do stars shoot water jets?

When stars are forming they can shoot out jets of material. Sometimes these jets have hydrogen and oxygen atoms, which make super-hot water that shoots into space!

REALLY COOL STUFF ABOUT SPACECRAFT

Spacecraft are amazing machines. Let's take a look at some more facts about these high-tech craft.

Can you see the pyramids from space?

The International Space Station orbits about 350 kilometres above Earth, and astronauts on board have used digital cameras to take pictures of the large pyramids in Giza, Egypt. But the farther away in space you go, the less you see on Earth. No human-made object on Earth can be seen from the Moon.

Why are spacesuits white?

Astronauts wear white spacesuits because white reflects heat and keeps the astronauts from getting too hot. White spacesuits are also easy to see against the black background of space, which means spacewalkers do not go missing!

How much space junk is there around the Earth?

There are lots of human-made bits orbiting Earth. This swarm of junk includes old satellites, pieces of rockets and even a screwdriver that slipped from the hand of an astronaut! There are nearly 500,000 pieces of space junk.

Why did a spacecraft crash into Jupiter?

In 2003, after many years studying the planet, a space probe called Galileo crashed into Jupiter. The probe had run out of fuel. It was crushed by the thick layers of gas around the giant planet.

How can gravity speed up a spacecraft?

Scientists use the gravity of the Sun and planets to make spacecraft move faster, like a catapult. The spacecraft are flown several times around a planet and then flung out towards its final path.

How long would a 747 jumbo jet take to fly to the Moon?

Planes can't fly to the Moon because there is no air in space to burn their fuel. If you did travel at the speed of a 747 jumbo jet, it would take nearly 18 days to get to the Moon!

Has an alien spaceship ever landed on the Earth?

Despite what we see in movies, no aliens have ever come to Earth. People see Unidentified Flying Objects (or UFOs), but most turn out to be normal things such as planes, clouds or the planet Venus!

Will there be a mission to the Sun?

No spacecraft has ever been closer to the Sun than the orbit of Mercury. But a new mission called Solar Probe is planned for launch in 2018 and will fly just 9 million kilometres above the surface of the Sun.

How hot does a rocket engine get?

It is very difficult to measure the temperature in the middle of a rocket engine that's in full blast. The main engines of the space shuttle burn at an amazing 3300 degrees Celsius and use up nearly 2 million tonnes of fuel in less than 9 minutes!

Are the footprints of astronauts still on the Moon?

The footprints of the astronauts who went to the Moon will be there for millions of years because there is no wind on the Moon to blow them away.

TOP 40 UNIVERSE FACTS

1. The most distant known galaxy, UDFj-39546284, is more than 13 billion light-years away from Earth.

2. IC1101 is the largest known galaxy, with a diameter of 5.5 million light-years.

3. At a distance of 17,000 light-years, Omega Centauri is the nearest galaxy to our Milky Way Galaxy.

4. The most energetic galaxy is Markarian 231, which has a super-massive black hole at its centre.

5. ISOHDFS 27 is the most massive spiral galaxy known, with a mass that is more than 1,000 billion times that of the Sun.

6. The brightest galaxy visible in the night sky is the Large Magellanic Cloud, about 150,000 light-years from Earth.

7. The spiral galaxy NGC 253 is the dustiest galaxy known, with a total amount of dust nearly 80 million times the mass of the Sun.

8. The quasar galaxy LBQS 1429-008 is really a triplet with three super-massive black holes squeezing together.

9. VIRGOHI21 is a galaxy where no stars shine. It is made entirely of invisible dark matter.

10. A record-breaking seven supernova stars have been seen exploding at the same time in the galaxy Arp 220. It is moving at nearly 5 million kilometres an hour.

11. Jupiter is the largest planet in the Solar System. Nearly 1320 Earths would fit inside Jupiter.

12. Saturn has the widest rings of any planet. The span of its rings is only slightly less than the distance between the Earth and Moon.

13. Jupiter is the fastest-spinning planet, turning once in just under ten hours.

14. Venus is the hottest planet, with a surface that can rise to 460 degrees Celsius – hot enough to melt lead!

15. Neptune has the fastest winds in the Solar System, reaching speeds of more than 2000 km per hour.

16. The Solar System's largest moon is Ganymede, which orbits Jupiter and is larger than the planet Mercury.

17. The tallest mountain in the solar system is Olympus Mons on Mars. It is nearly three times higher than Mount Everest on Earth.

18. Venus is the brightest planet we can see in the night sky.

19. Neptune is the coldest planet of our Solar System, with temperatures that can drop to -200 degrees Celsius.

20. There are more active volcanoes and earthquakes on Earth than any other planet in the Solar System.

21. The brightest star in the night sky is Sirius.

22. The nearest star to the Sun is over four light-years away and is called Proxima Centauri.

23. The most magnetic star is a magnetar 1E 2259+586. It is more magnetic than 100-trillion fridge magnets!

24. The largest known star is VY Canis Majoris and it is 2100 times larger than the Sun.

25. The fastest-spinning star is PSR J1748-2446ad. It spins 716 times every second.

26. The largest known star R136a1 has 265 times more mass than the Sun.

27. The hottest known star at 220,000 degrees Celsius is a white dwarf called NGC 6302.

28. The most powerful known star LBV 1806-20 is 40 million times more powerful than the Sun.

29. The most distant supernova seen was 5 billion light-years away and is named ESO8802.

30. The fastest moving star is a neutron star known as RX J0822-4300. It is moving at nearly 5 million kilometres an hour.

31. The tallest rocket ever was *Saturn 5*, which took astronauts to the Moon. *Saturn 5* was 110 metres tall, which is higher than a 30-storey building!

32. The fastest spacecraft is the *New Horizons* mission to Pluto. It moves at nearly 60,000 kilometres per hour.

33. The longest spacewalk lasted 8 hours and 56 minutes outside the International Space Station.

34. The most reused spacecraft is the space shuttle *Discovery*, which flew 38 times.

35. The *Mars Odyssey* spacecraft is the longest-working orbiter. It first started orbiting Mars in October 2001.

36. The farthest place a spacecraft has ever touched down is Saturn's giant moon Titan, visited by the *Huygens* lander.

37. The coldest working spacecraft is *Planck*, the scientific instruments of which are kept just above –273 degrees Celsius!

38. At 17.5 billion kilometres, *Voyager 1* is the most distant spacecraft from Earth.

39. The largest space crew ever was when 8 astronauts were launched on the *Challenger* space shuttle.

40. The *Galileo* spacecraft made the fastest entry into an atmosphere. It entered Jupiter's gas layers at nearly 170,000 kilometres per hour!

USEFUL WEBSITES

Hubble Space Telescope Gallery
http://hubblesite.org/gallery

European Space Agency http://
www.esa.int

BBC Space http://www.bbc.co.uk/
science/space/

NASA http://www.nasa.gov/audience/
forkids/kidsclub/flash/index.html

National Geographic Space
http://science.nationalgeographic.com/
science/space/

Online Star Map http://www.open2.
net/science/finalfrontier/planisphere/
planisphere_embedded.html

Astronomy Picture of the Day
http://apod.nasa.gov/apod/

GLOSSARY

ammonia A smelly chemical made from hydrogen and nitrogen.

antenna A large dish that can send or receive radio signals.

asteroid A space rock. Most asteroids orbit in a belt between Mars and Jupiter.

astronaut A person who travels in space.

astronomer A scientist who studies objects in space, such as planets, stars and galaxies.

atmosphere The gases that surround a planet or moon.

atoms Tiny building blocks that makes up all matter.

bacteria Tiny life forms, sometimes known as germs.

Big Bang A theory that says the Universe began with an enormously powerful explosion.

Big Crunch The idea that the Universe will start to get smaller and smaller and eventually collapse.

Big Freeze The idea that in the future the Universe may get colder as it grows larger and end up with no heat at all.

Big Rip A possible ending of the Universe in which all matter, including planets, stars and galaxies, are pulled apart.

billion A very large number written as 1 followed by 9 zeros.

black hole A region of space around a very small and very heavy object inside which the gravity is so strong that nothing, not even light, can escape from it.

brown dwarf A space object that has hardly any mass and doesn't make light that we can see.

comet An icy body with an orbit that brings it close to the Sun at regular intervals.

constellation An imaginary pattern drawn between different stars.

core The central part of an object, such as a planet or star.

cosmic To do with the Cosmos, another word for Universe.

day The amount of time it takes for a planet to spin around once. Earth's day is 24 hours, but Venus's is 243 Earth days!

dust (in space) Tiny grains of solid particles found between stars.

Earth's crust The shell of rocks that surrounds our planet.

element A pure chemical, such as hydrogen, oxygen, carbon or nitrogen.

equator The imaginary line that divides a planet into a northern and southern half.

exoplanet A planet that orbits a star that is not the Sun.

galaxy Collection of stars, gas and dust held together by gravity.

gamma rays High-energy rays that are made by the hottest objects in the Universe.

gravity A force that attracts two objects and which depends on the amount of matter in the objects and their distance apart.

helium A chemical element that is made inside stars when hydrogen atoms join together.

hurricane A powerful storm with strong winds.

hydrogen A chemical element that is found inside stars. It is the smallest, lightest and most common element in the universe.

hypernova The most powerful explosion known in the Universe.

infrared Light of low energy that is invisible but can be felt as heat.

lander A space vehicle that is designed to land on the surface of a moon or planet.

lens A curved piece of glass that can be used to bend rays of light.

light-year The distance light can travel in one year, which is 9000 billion kilometres.

matter Anything that has mass and makes up an object.

Mir A space station built by Russia and launched in 1986. It was the first space station to be permanently occupied by cosmonauts. Some cosmonauts spent over a year on Mir.

nebula Clouds of gas and dust in space. New stars are made here.

neutron star A very tightly packed dead star formed after a supernova.

nuclear fusion A process where small atoms are pushed together to make a heavier one releasing huge amounts of energy.

orbit The path that a planet takes around the Sun. Orbits are oval in shape.

planet A large object, such as Earth, that orbits a star.

planetary nebula A cloud of gas seen surrounding stars the size of the Sun when they run out of energy and begin to die.

quasar A very powerful and distant galaxy that puts out lots of light.

red giant A small star that has swollen to a much larger size than the Sun is today.

rover A space vehicle used to explore the surface of a moon or planet. A rover can have a crew or it can be controlled from Earth.

solar system Our Solar System is the Sun and the planets, moons and other space objects that travel around it.

space shuttle A space vehicle that took off like a rocket and landed like an aeroplane and carried people into space. There were 135 space shuttle missions between 1981 and 2011, when the shuttle programme ended.

spacecraft A vehicle for travel beyond the Earth's atmosphere.

spiral A pinwheel shape.

supercluster Made of groups of galaxies that are linked together and stretch for hundreds of millions of light-years.

supernova A violent event that happens when massive stars explode.

telescope A device using lenses and mirrors for viewing objects that are far away.

temperature A measure of how much heat is inside something.

thrust Force that pushes down when a rocket burns its engines.

trillion A huge number written as 1 followed by 12 zeros.

Universe The huge space which contains all of time, matter and energy.

volcanoes Openings in a planet's surface through which hot liquid rock is thrown up.

white dwarf A very hot and small object that forms when medium-sized stars like the Sun run out of energy and die.

X-rays A type of high-energy light that can pass through most solid objects.

year The amount of time it takes for a planet to go around the Sun. Earth's year is 365 days but every other planet's year is different.

INDEX